LAUGHTER
THE BEST MEDICINE™
THOSE LOVABLE PETS

LAUGHTER
THE BEST MEDICINE™
THOSE LOVABLE PETS

America's Funniest Jokes, Quotes, and Cartoons

Reader's
Digest

The Reader's Digest Association, Inc.
New York, NY/Montreal

A READER'S DIGEST BOOK

FOR READER'S DIGEST
Project Designer: Elizabeth Tunnicliffe
Manager, English Book Editorial, Reader's Digest Canada: Pamela Johnson
Senior Art Director: George McKeon
Executive Editor, Trade Publishing: Dolores York
Manufacturing Manager: Elizabeth Dinda
Associate Publisher, Trade Publishing: Rosanne McManus
President and Publisher, Trade Publishing: Harold Clarke

Library of Congress Cataloging-in-Publication Data

Laughter is the best medicine : those lovable pets.
    p. cm.
  ISBN 978-1-60652-357-5
  1. Animals--Humor. 2. Pets--Humor. I. Reader's Digest Association.
  PN6231.A5L38 2012
  818'.60208--dc23
                            2011033163

Cover and spot illustrations: George McKeon
Cartoon Credits: Ian Baker: *76;* John Caldwell: *10, 44, 118, 176, 197;* Dave Carpenter: *55, 63, 141,
165, 173, 208;* Joe di Chiarro: *205;* Roy Delgado: *15, 33, 93, 104, 128;* Ralph Hagen: *111;*
Mike Lynch: *133, 139, 144, 159, 182;* Scott Arthur Masear: *28, 49;* Harley Schwadron: *20, 96, 154;*
Steve Smeltzer: *25, 68, 168, 192;* Thomas Bros.: *73, 123, 136, 149;* Kim Warp: *41, 58, 187;*
WestMach: *36, 81, 200*

We are committed to both the quality of our products and the service we provide to
our customers. We value your comments, so please feel free to contact us.

            The Reader's Digest Association, Inc.
            Adult Trade Publishing
            44 S. Broadway
            White Plains, NY 10601

For more Reader's Digest products and information, visit our website:

            www.rd.com (in the United States)
            www.readersdigest.ca (in Canada)

Printed in the United States of America

3 5 7 9 10 8 6 4

♥ ♥ ♥ ♥ ♥ ♥ ♥ ♥ ♥ ♥ ♥ ♥

Contents

♥ ♥ ♥ ♥ ♥ ♥ ♥ ♥ ♥ ♥ ♥

A Note from the Editors

People are funny, but so are the animals we love—and our day-to-day relationships with them can be even more entertaining. From cats fined for littering to dogs that tremble at the sight of their own "Beware of Dog" sign, this book is dedicated to the companions we hold so dear—our pets.

And it doesn't just stop with cats and dogs. Sure, these furry friends rule the comedic roost, but within the pages of *Laughter Is the Best Medicine: Those Lovable Pets,* parrots, bunnies, hamsters, and even the occasional white rat are an endless source of amusement as well. Take, for instance, the scientist who crossed the carrier pigeon with a woodpecker and got a bird that not only delivered its message to the home of the designated recipient but also knocked on the door when it got there!

By way of funny tales, quotes, and cartoons compiled from more than eight decades' worth of *Reader's Digest* magazine, this book brings to life the often funny relationships we have with our animals—and promises to make you laugh your tail off.

To the
dogs

I think dogs are the most amazing creatures; they give unconditional love. For me they are the role model for being alive.

—GILDA RADNER

"Honey, the dog learned a new trick and now I owe him twelve dollars."

♥ ♥ ♥ ♥ ♥ ♥ ♥ ♥ ♥ ♥ ♥

I keep five dogs in my backyard, in four houses of various sizes. One day, during a heavy rainstorm, I went out to check on my pets. The big house was occupied by one dog, the middle-sized house held two, and the small houses had one pet each. Satisfied that they were all snug and dry, I left. A little later lightning streaked across the sky and thunder boomed. When I peeked out the back door, all the houses were empty except the big one. In it were all five dogs.

—JUNE CROSSLAND

Our happy little fox terrier, Cookie, had a game all her own. Every time we climbed into our car, she took a head start to race us to the bottom of the hill. Down the driveway she would scoot, across our near-neighbor's lawn, down the hill, across a basketball court, through a little gate, around our new neighbor's house, and through her front hedge just in time to grin at us as we caught up a half block from home.

Our new neighbor down the hill, upon meeting us for the first time recently, remarked, "We always know when you folks are going somewhere."

"How can you tell?" I asked.

"Well," she said, "it's strange, but always just before you drive past our house, our cat climbs a tree."

—MRS. W. T. BOONE

Our daughter was working as a telemarketer for a home-security firm. Once while she was reciting all the benefits of the system to a potential customer, he interrupted her and said, "We don't need it because we have a big dog."

"That's great," my daughter replied. "But can he dial 911?"

—EVELYNE DREEBEN

♥ ♥ ♥ ♥ ♥ ♥ ♥ ♥ ♥ ♥ ♥

"For sale: **Eight puppies from a German shepherd and an Alaskan hussy.**"

—RICHARD A. HARMS

Driving to work one morning, I heard an announcement on the radio about a lost dog. The deejay said the owner was offering a cash reward for its return. Getting to the traffic segment of his broadcast, the deejay asked the helicopter pilot who monitors morning rush hour what the roads were like. "To heck with the traffic," the pilot said on the air, "we're going to look for that dog!"

—SUZANNE DOPP

I'm a police officer and occasionally park my cruiser in residential areas to watch for speeders. One Sunday morning I was staked out in a driveway, when I saw a large dog trot up to my car. He stopped and sat just out of arm's reach. No matter how much I tried to coax him to come for a pat on the head, he refused to budge. After a while I decided to move to another location. I pulled out of the driveway, looked back and learned the reason for the dog's stubbornness. He quickly picked up the newspaper I had been parked on and dutifully ran back to his master.

—JEFF WALL

I was in a bank when a man entered with a rather large dog on a leash. When he asked if it was okay to bring his pet into the building, a bank official answered, "Yes, providing he doesn't make a deposit."

—JOHN REED

♥ ♥ ♥ ♥ ♥ ♥ ♥ ♥ ♥ ♥ ♥

The drive-up window at the bank where I'm a teller has an outside drawer to accept customer transactions. A woman once drove up with her dog in the front seat, and the pet eagerly jumped over onto the driver's lap when the car reached my window. He looked excited to see me. "Your dog is so friendly!" I said to the owner.

"He thinks he's at McDonald's," she replied.

—MARILYN BOURDEAU

As a mail carrier in Florida, I was attempting to deliver a certified letter when I heard a dog barking furiously on the other side of a front door. I stepped away from the door as the homeowner appeared, and asked that the dog be kept inside. It was too late. The little dog started yelping and jumping on me. I froze. As the customer signed for his letter, he kept saying, "Don't worry, he won't bite you." Just then the dog turned and bit its owner.

—RAMONA OCCHIUZZO

Whenever the alarm goes off after-hours at the municipal office where I work, the security company calls me at home and I have to go back and reset it. Late at night I got one of those calls. As I was getting ready to head out the door, my husband groggily said, "You're not going down there by yourself at this hour." Just as I was thinking, How thoughtful of him, he added, **"Better take the dog with you."**

—RUTH RODDICK

❤ ❤ ❤ ❤ ❤ ❤ ❤ ❤ ❤ ❤ ❤

A new restaurant near our office boasted exotic fare. And exotic it was. When our dessert arrived, my coworker sniffed her chocolate dish and grimaced. "It smells like cocoa," she said.

"It's chocolate—shouldn't it smell like cocoa?" I asked.

More confused than I was, she answered, "Cocoa is the name of my dog."

—CYNTHIA ZHANG

My sister-in-law, a truck driver, had decided to get a dog for protection. As she inspected a likely candidate, the trainer told her, "He doesn't like men."

Perfect, my sister-in-law thought, and took the dog. Then one day she was approached by two men in a parking lot, and she watched to see how her canine bodyguard would react. Soon it became clear that the trainer wasn't kidding. As the men got closer, the dog ran under the nearest car.

—DANNY ARIAIL

My wife found this flyer taped to a neighborhood telephone pole:

"Found, male yellow Lab, very friendly. Loves to play with kids and eat Bubbles. Bubbles is our cat. Please come get your dog."

—ROBERT CHAPMAN

What's the difference between a man and a dog running?

One wears trousers and the other pants.

MARIE TERRIEN

"When are you getting the windshield wipers fixed, Harold?"

Who could resist this sales pitch my ten-year-old daughter, Courtney, gave, describing what her future would be like. She told me she would have three dogs.

"Why three?" I asked.

Courtney said that when she slept, she'd have one big dog to rest her head on like a pillow, and a small one cuddled under each arm.

"Oh," I replied, "So if you're in bed with the three dogs around you and in your arms, what about your husband?"

Courtney was quiet for a moment as she thought this through. Finally she said, "He can get his own dog!"

—WALLY VOGEL

♥ ♥ ♥ ♥ ♥ ♥ ♥ ♥ ♥ ♥ ♥

Our dog, a Shih Tzu, was missing, and we
advertised on the radio and in the paper.
Several days later, a woman called.

"I think I have your dog," she told my wife,
"but I don't know what a Shih Tzu looks like."

"Point your finger at the animal
and say, **'Bang!'"** my wife told her.

In a few minutes the woman was back on the line.
"The dog fell over," she reported.

We had found our pet.

—BILL MORRIS

Friends of mine sold their country home to move to the city
after arranging for the new owners to keep their dog that they
said was an excellent watch dog.

On their first night in the city, they received a frantic phone
call from the new owners. "Please come back and collect your
dog," they begged. "We've been out for the day and it won't let
us back onto the property."

—NORMA KAWAK

♥ ♥ ♥ ♥ ♥ ♥ ♥ ♥ ♥ ♥ ♥

At the end of the day, I parked my police van in front of the station house. My K-9 partner, Jake, was in the back barking, which caught the attention of a boy who was passing by. "Is that a dog you have back there?" he asked.

"It sure is," I said.

"What did he do?"

—CLINT FORWARD

A man and his dog entered the hardware store where I work. The man turned right, toward housewares. The dog turned left, toward pet supplies. The man returned to the checkout counter with kitchen tiling. The dog returned to the checkout counter with a fleece toy. The man paid for both, and they left, each carrying his own item.

—KENT MILLER

Once while riding the bus to work, I noticed a man at a stop enjoying a cup of coffee.

As we approached the stop, he finished drinking and set the cup on the ground. This negligence surprised me, since it seemed to be a good ceramic cup.

Days later I saw the same man again drinking his coffee at the bus stop. Once again, he placed the cup on the grass before boarding. When the bus pulled away, I looked back in time to see a dog carefully carrying the cup in his mouth as he headed for home.

—VALERIE A. HUEBNER

❤ ❤ ❤ ❤ ❤ ❤ ❤ ❤ ❤ ❤ ❤

I was editing classified ads for a small-town newspaper when a man called to place an ad.

"It should read," he said, "'Free to good home. Golden retriever. Will eat anything, loves children.'"

—ELLEN YOUNG

Recently, my husband and I went to the movies. When the film ended, we sat for a few minutes discussing how disappointing it was. When we stood up, we overheard another couple having the same discussion. The man said, "For that we left the dog alone at home?"

—LOIS DAVIS IN *THE NEW YORK TIMES*

I had just come out of a store when the blast of a car horn scared me. When I turned to yell at the rude driver, I found a large white poodle sitting in the driver's seat of a parked car. When the impatient dog honked again, a man came scurrying out of a shop, shouting, "I'll be there in a minute!"

"Did you teach your dog to do that?" I asked the man.

"Yes," he answered in exasperation, "and now he won't let me go anywhere!"

—NANCY E. HAIGH

A truck ran a red light, almost sideswiping our car. As my husband veered away, he threw his arm across me, protecting me from a possible collision. I was ready to plant a big kiss on my hero's cheek when he apologized. In his haste, he admitted, he had forgotten it was me in the front seat and not our black Labrador, Checkers.

—APRIL COLE

QUOTABLE QUOTES

"So many of Lassie's fans want to ask: Is he allowed on the furniture? Of course he is—but then, he's the one who paid for it."

—JULIA GLASS

"I dressed my dog up as a cat for Halloween. Now he won't come when I call him."

—ROOFTOP COMEDY

"Dogs don't bark at parked cars."

—LYNNE CHENEY

"You own a dog; you feed a cat."

—JIM FIEBIG

"Don't accept your dog's admiration as conclusive evidence that you are wonderful."

—ANN LANDERS

"We give dogs time we can spare, space we can spare, and love we can spare. In return, dogs give us their all. It's the best deal man has ever made."

—MARGERY FACKLAM, AUTHOR

One dog to another: "What if the hand that feeds us is surprisingly tasty?"

—PETE MUELLER IN *BARK*

"If dogs could talk, it would take a lot of fun out of owning one."

— ANDREW A. ROONEY, FROM *NOT THAT YOU ASKED* (RANDOM HOUSE)

"I wonder if other dogs think poodles are members of a weird religious cult."

—RITA RUDNER

"He's a high-tech watchdog."

❤ ❤ ❤ ❤ ❤ ❤ ❤ ❤ ❤ ❤ ❤

My friend has a golden retriever that responds to music, and seems to especially like opera. The dog is appropriately named Poochini.

—JERRY SIMON

My sister's dog had been deaf and blind for years. When she started to suffer painful tumors, it was time to put her down. As I explained this to my seven-year-old son, he asked if Jazzy would go to heaven. I said I thought she would, and that in dog heaven, she would be healthy again and able to do her favorite thing: chase squirrels. Jacob thought about that for a minute then said, "So dog heaven must be the same as squirrel hell."

—JUDY SUTTERFIELD

As the stranger enters a country store, he spots a sign: "Danger! Beware of Dog!" Inside, he sees a harmless old hound asleep in the middle of the floor. "Is that the dog we're supposed to beware of?" he asks the owner.

"That's him," comes the reply.

"He doesn't look dangerous to me. Why would you post that sign?"

"Before I posted that sign, people kept tripping over him."

—L. B. WEINSTEIN

A French poodle and a collie were walking down the street. The poodle turned to the collie and complained, "My life is such a mess. My owner is mean, my girlfriend is having an affair with a German shepherd and I'm as nervous as a cat."

"Why don't you go see a psychiatrist?" asked the collie.

"I can't," replied the poodle. "I'm not allowed on the couch."

—JOHN W. GAMBA

♥ ♥ ♥ ♥ ♥ ♥ ♥ ♥ ♥ ♥

Did you ever notice that when you blow in a dog's face he gets mad at you, but when you take him on a car ride, he sticks his head out the window

—ROBYN CAMPBELL-OUCHIDA

Why It's Great to be a Dog
- No one expects you to take a bath every day.
- If it itches, you can scratch it.
- There's no such thing as bad food.
- A rawhide bone can entertain you for hours.
- If you grow hair in weird places, no one notices.
- You can lie around all day without worrying about being fired.
- You don't get in trouble for putting your head in a stranger's lap.
- You're always excited to see the same people.
- Having big feet is considered an asset.
- Puppy love can last.

—DAWN DRESSLER FROM *THE SUN*, BREMERTON WASHINGTON

We were going out of state for six weeks and asked the neighbors' nine-year-old son, Mike, to care for our dog. We explained that the job required feeding, grooming, walking and, most of all, plenty of love and playtime. Then we asked Mike what the job would be worth to him.

"I'll give you ten bucks," he said.

—JOAN KLINGLER

 What do you get when you cross a chili pepper, a shovel and a chihuahua?

A hot diggity dog.

These guys, one a pessimist and the other an eternal optimist, had been friends for years. The optimist was always trying to get his pal to see the bright side of things. The optimist found a dog that could walk on water. This is perfect, he thought. There's no way that darn cynic can say anything negative about this. He took his friend duck hunting so he could see the dog in action. Mid-morning, they finally downed a bird. It fell on the other side of the lake, so the optimist sent the dog to retrieve it. The animal trotted across the water, grabbed the duck in his mouth, and ran back. "Isn't that amazing?"

"Hmmph," the cynic said. "That dog can't swim, can it?"

With a young child on the stand, the district attorney knew he needed to start with some simple questions. "If I were to tell you that this pen was red, would that be the truth or a lie?" he asked.

"The truth," said the child.

"Very good!" said the D.A. "And if I were to say that dogs could talk, would that be the truth or a lie?"

"The truth," said the child again.

"Really?" asked the D.A. "Dogs can talk? What do they say?"

"I don't know," the child answered. "I don't talk dog."

—LOS ANGELES COUNTY SUPERIOR COURT COMMISSIONER
MICHAEL A. COWELL IN *LOS ANGELES DAILY JOURNAL*

♥ ♥ ♥ ♥ ♥ ♥ ♥ ♥ ♥ ♥ ♥

An engineer, an accountant, a chemist and a bureaucrat are bragging about how smart their dogs are. The engineer called to his dog, "T-Square, do your stuff." The dog took out paper and pen and drew a circle, a square, and a triangle. Everyone agreed he was smart.

The accountant called, "Slide Rule, do your stuff." The pooch went to the kitchen, got a dozen cookies and made four stacks of three. Everyone was impressed.

The chemist called, "Beaker, do your stuff." The dog went to the fridge for a quart of milk, got a ten-ounce glass and poured exactly eight ounces without spilling a drop. Everyone agreed that was great.

The bureaucrat called, "Coffee Break, do your stuff!" Coffee Break ate the cookies, drank the milk, chewed the paper, claimed he injured his mouth doing so, filed a grievance for unsafe work conditions, put in for Workers' Compensation and took extended sick leave.

A Great Dane, a Scottie and a chihuahua were sitting in a bar, knocking back a few, when a beautiful French poodle walked in.

"Hi, boys," she said seductively, "I'll make a very happy dog out of whichever of you comes up with the best proposition using the words cheese and liver."

The Great Dane thought for a moment, and then declared, "I don't like cheese, but I sure like liver, and I like you, too!" The lady just looked away, obviously unimpressed. The Scottie immediately followed with, "I like cheese, and I like liver, and I like you!" He wagged his tail expectantly, but she ignored him.

Then the chihuahua stepped forward. "Liver alone!" he growled. "Cheese with me!" They left together.

" Word to the wise: Always check the cheese for pills. "

An on-duty policeman and another gentleman were both interested in adopting the same dog at the SPCA where I work. I told both customers that they'd have to draw for the pet. The uniformed officer stepped back from the counter, put his hand on his hip just above his service revolver and with a grin drawled, "That suits me just fine."

—RICHARD A. CROOKES

♥ ♥ ♥ ♥ ♥ ♥ ♥ ♥ ♥ ♥ ♥

This ad in the *Bozeman Daily Chronicle* was obviously directed toward pet lovers only: **"Free to good home, a loving Jack Russell terror dog."**

—SARAH RUEFER

Because our dog, Dakota, travels with us in the car, my husband and I give him sugarless mints to sweeten his doggy breath. Soon he developed a taste for them. One day while my husband and I were out in the country, we let Dakota run off-leash. He began wandering away. I yelled for him to stop, stay, come. He ignored me and kept running. Finally, unable to think of anything else, I shouted, "Who wants a breath mint?" He stopped dead in his tracks.

—SUSAN NELSON

Driving back from Vermont, I stopped at a vegetable stand. It was deserted except for a sleeping German shepherd. I stepped over the dog, helped myself to some corn, then opened the cashbox to pay. Taped to the inside of the lid was this note: "The dog can count."

—CARLEEN CRUMMETT

One year on vacation I went to a resort in Wyoming. As part of the usual activities, a neighboring ranch invited guests from our resort to participate in a cattle drive. After watching 20 make-believe cowpokes whooping and hollering, I rode up to the ranch owner and asked her how many cowboys it normally takes to drive a herd of that size.

"One," she replied, "and a dog."

—DEBORAH BLITZ

A couple of dog owners are arguing about whose pet is smarter. "My dog is so smart," says the first owner, "that every morning he waits for the paperboy to come around. He tips the kid and then brings the newspaper to me, along with my morning coffee."

"I know," says the second owner.

"How do you know?"

"My dog told me."

—SOURABH BHATIA

I dressed up my dog as a mailman for Halloween. He bit himself.

—CHRISTINA MELTON

Two dogs were out for a walk. One dog says to the other, "Wait here a minute. I'll be right back." He walks across the street and sniffs a fire hydrant for about a minute, then rejoins his friend. "What was that all about?" the other dog asks.

"Just checking my messages."

My dog plopped into my lap, accidentally speed-dialing an emergency number on the cell phone in my pocket. Moments later the phone rang. "This is Dallas Fire and Rescue. We received a call from this number. Is everything okay?"

Quickly I realized what had happened. "I'm fine. My dog must have punched your number."

The voice on the other end inquired, **"And how is your dog?"**

—CONSTANCE STROW

❤ ❤ ❤ ❤ ❤ ❤ ❤ ❤ ❤ ❤ ❤

"He's a power pointer."

Irate man with dog, to pet-shop owner: "Of all the nerve! You sold me this mutt as a watchdog. Yesterday a robber broke into my home and stole three hundred dollars, and the miserable animal didn't make a sound."

Pet-shop owner: "My dear sir, this dog used to belong to very wealthy people. He doesn't react to such small amounts."

—FRITZ HERDI

♥ ♥ ♥ ♥ ♥ ♥ ♥ ♥ ♥ ♥ ♥

During their observance of Animal Week, the fourth-graders told about their kindnesses to pets. Asked what he had done, one little boy said: "I kicked a boy for kicking his dog."

—MARY WRIGHT

I was shopping in the pet section of my local supermarket when I overheard a woman singing the praises of a particular water bowl to her husband. "Look, it even has a water filter!" she concluded, holding the doggie dish out for her husband's inspection. He had a slightly different take on things: "Dear, he drinks out of the toilet."

—JAMES JENKINS

Butch, our boxer, hated taking his medicine. After a lot of trial and error my father eventually figured out the simplest way to get it into him: blow it down Butch's throat with something called a pill tube. So Dad put the large tablet in one end of the tube, forced the reluctant dog's jaws open, and poked the other end into his mouth. Then, just as my father inhaled to blow, Butch coughed.

A startled look appeared on Dad's face. He opened his eyes wide and swallowed hard. "I think I've just been de-wormed," he gasped.

—JOHN ROBERTSON

Why are dogs such bad dancers?
They have two left feet.

❤ ❤ ❤ ❤ ❤ ❤ ❤ ❤ ❤ ❤

The 6 a.m. regulars at the dog run are, not surprisingly, a pet-oriented group.

Recently John started discussing his trip. "The flight was awful! We were delayed for a few hours, and when we finally boarded, the baby behind me didn't stop crying for the whole flight."

Another dog-run regular turned to him in surprise: "What did the owner do?"

—TOBY YOUNG

The Doggie Diner in Bellingham, Wash., has grossed $10,000 a month since opening last year. The eatery is so popular that reservations are a must for parties of more than two dogs. And, yes, the patrons are strictly canine. Says co-owner Taimi Gorham, "If a cat comes in, he's on his own. "

—THE CHRISTIAN SCIENCE MONITOR

On the last day of school, the children brought gifts for the teacher. The florist's son brought the teacher a bouquet. The candy-store owner's daughter handed the teacher a pretty box of candy. Then the liquor-store owner's son brought up a big, heavy box. The teacher lifted it up and noticed that it was leaking a little bit. She touched a drop of the liquid with her finger and tasted it.

"Is it wine?" she guessed.

"No," the boy replied.

She tasted another drop and asked, "Champagne?"

"No," said the little boy.

"I give up," she said.

"What is it?"

"A puppy!"

♥ ♥ ♥ ♥ ♥ ♥ ♥ ♥ ♥ ♥ ♥

When I was ill, my husband and I were stuck in the house for months. But I made a complete recovery and was so happy the day he bounded into the kitchen and asked, "Would you like to go out, girl?"

"I'd love to," I replied immediately.

We had a wonderful meal, culminating with my husband making a confession. "Remember when I suggested going out tonight?" he asked.

"Yes," I said.

"I was talking to the dog."

—ANITA SAUNDERS

Although legally declared blind, my friend Walter is able to see shadows, so he enjoys watching television. One day he was engrossed in one of his favorite programs when Joey, his guide dog, let him know that she needed to go out. "Okay, Joey, as soon as this program's over." She waited a few minutes, and then nudged his knee. "Wait until the program's over," Walter said impatiently. Joey sat a few more minutes, looking from Walter to the screen. Then she nudged him again and whined briefly. When Walter continued to ignore her, Joey calmly walked around behind the television, grasped the electric cord in her mouth, and unplugged the set.

—FLORENCE M. WEEKES

♥ ♥ ♥ ♥ ♥ ♥ ♥ ♥ ♥ ♥

"I've really had it with my dog. He'll chase anyone on a bike."
"So what are you going to do—leave him at the pound?
Sell him?"
"No, nothing that drastic. I think I'll just take his bike away."

I arrived home from work to find all the windows and doors wide open. Apparently our puppy had had an accident.

"Yeah, it really stank," my daughter told me. "In fact, when we first walked in, I thought you had come home early and were cooking dinner."

—TIMOTHY SCOTT FOUBERT

After I completed a frantic afternoon of chores, I walked into the living room to find my husband reclining in his chair. He was looking bemusedly at our new puppy, who was napping.

"If I wanted to look at something lying around sleeping all day," he complained, "I would have bought a cat."

"Or you could have just bought a mirror," I said.

—TRACEY SMITH

We got a new dog, a dachshund. Next came the big question: what to call him. The winner came from our son, Brian.

"Hypotenuse," he suggested. Why? "He's got a long side between two shorter legs."

—JENNY ROWE

"If I had a cellphone you wouldn't have to whistle all the time."

QUOTABLE QUOTES

"A dog is the only thing on earth that loves you more than you love yourself."

—JOSH BILLINGS

"The dog is mentioned in the Bible eighteen times—the cat not even once."

—W. E. FARBSTEIN

"If your dog is fat, you aren't getting enough exercise."

—UNKNOWN

"Did you ever walk into a room and forget why you walked in? I think that's how dogs spend their lives."

—SUE MURPHY

"If you are a dog and your owner suggests that you wear a sweater... suggest that he wear a tail."

—FRAN LEBOWITZ

"The dog is a yes-animal, very popular with people who can't afford to keep a yes-man."

—ROBERTSON DAVIES

"A dog is the only exercise machine you cannot decide to skip when you don't feel like it."

—CAROLYN G. HEILBRUN
IN *THE LAST GIFT OF TIME*

"Dogs feel very strongly that they should always go with you in the car, in case the need should arise for them to bark violently at nothing right in your ear."

—DAVE BARRY IN *MIAMI HERALD*

♥ ♥ ♥ ♥ ♥ ♥ ♥ ♥ ♥ ♥

Whenever my family leaves the house, our Shetland sheepdog's animal instincts start to kick in. He runs circles around us and nips at our heels to keep us all together. Watching this display, my friend couldn't resist: "You always herd the ones you love."

—JOLENE HUEHOLT

Brownie was the last of a litter of pups in the window of the pet shop where I work. Although his looks were nondescript and he wasn't even a puppy anymore, his tail wagged jauntily, hopefully, at anyone who stopped to look. On the day that Brownie was to be transferred to the city pound, a pleasant young woman with several children in tow came in and bought him.

"I suppose it's an advertising gimmick," she said, "but it really got me."

I understood what she meant when I went to pull the "For Sale" sticker off the window. Someone had changed the 'l' to 'k' and added an 'n.'

—MARGARET WARK

My husband took our dog to the veterinarian and sat in the waiting room with the other dog owners. Suddenly the street door opened a few inches and an authoritative voice called, "Better get a tight hold on your animals!"

Everyone grasped his pet protectively, nervously wondering what sort of brute was to be led in. The door opened slowly— and in walked the mailman. He dropped some letters on a table, grinned, and walked out.

—MRS. ROY J. OLSEN

"Sometimes, you just have to let the stick go."

❤ ❤ ❤ ❤ ❤ ❤ ❤ ❤ ❤ ❤ ❤

Recently I ran into an old friend who told me he was trying to find a home for his Boston terrier. He was moving, and pets were not allowed in his new apartment. Since I had been thinking of getting a pet for my family, I agreed to take the dog.

"Fine," said Bill, happily, "I'll give you all her personal effects, too."

The next afternoon a friend of Bill's arrived at my home, explaining that Bill and his family had already moved. He then produced the terrier and her personal effects: chain, dish, collar—and three puppies!

—JAMES R. FINCH

A friend of mine, scheduled to move from Dunedin, New Zealand, to Sydney, Australia, sent his pet golden retriever ahead by air, and asked the kennel owner to let him know as soon as the animal arrived. He was relieved to receive a cable the next morning with the simple message: "Woof, Woof."

—JOHN MACKIE

During our show and tell period in the third grade, Mike mentioned that his pet beagle was expecting puppies. From then on, the class eagerly awaited the news of their birth. When the day arrived, Mike announced glumly, "Well, they're here." It was obvious that he was disappointed, but because of the intense interest of the class in the pups, I asked, "What's wrong, Mike? Tell us more."

"Well," he said, "I wanted a collie, and my sister wanted a poodle, but all we got were beagles—and we already have a beagle."

—NANCY NABBEFELD

❤ ❤ ❤ ❤ ❤ ❤ ❤ ❤ ❤ ❤ ❤

In a pet shop: **"Don't say 'no' until you look the puppy in the eye."**

At a workshop on dog temperament, the instructor noted that a test for a canine's disposition was for an owner to fall down and act hurt. A dog with poor temperament would try to bite the person, whereas a good dog would lick his owner's face or show concern.

Once, while eating pizza in the living room, I decided to try out this theory on my two dogs. I stood up, clutched my heart, let out a scream and collapsed on the floor.

The dogs looked at me, glanced at each other and raced to the coffee table for my pizza.

—SUSAN MOTTICE

I gave my daughter-in-law a Pekingese puppy from my dog's litter. She tried to find an Oriental-sounding name for the pet, and since my son is an attorney, she thought she had succeeded admirably when she came up with So-Su-Mi.

—JUDY CHARUHAS

As a teacher in an inner-city school, I found that one of my end-of-year activities was to take my class to a park for a day of fun. My 185-pound Great Dane came with us. The children were amazed by what was probably the largest dog they'd ever seen, and they bombarded me with questions: "Does he bite?" "How much did he cost?" One student asked, "What does he eat?"

Before I could answer, a boy shouted, "Man, whatever he wants!"

—BARBARA E. DOYLE

♥ ♥ ♥ ♥ ♥ ♥ ♥ ♥ ♥ ♥ ♥

Our new cairn terrier weighed only three pounds, but he kept trying to run large dogs out of our yard with his tiny growls. We soon hit upon the appropriate name for him—Genghis Cairn.

—ANNE COFFIN YOUNG

My dog is half pit bull, half poodle. It's not much of a watchdog, but it's a vicious gossip.

—CRAIG SHOEMAKER

Ever notice the similarities between man and man's best friend?
• Both take up too much space on the bed.
• Both have irrational fears about vacuuming.
• Neither tells you what's bothering him.
• Neither of them notices when you get your hair cut.
• Neither understands what you see in cats.

—M. D. ROSENBERG/FROM *FUNNY TIMES*

My father and a friend were talking about the doors they had installed so their animals could let themselves in and out of the house. My dad asked his friend, who had two massive Great Danes, "Aren't you afraid that somebody might crawl through the dogs' door and steal something?"

"If you saw an opening that big," said his friend, "would you crawl through it?"

—HORST JENKINS

❤ ❤ ❤ ❤ ❤ ❤ ❤ ❤ ❤ ❤ ❤

The dog owner claimed that his pet, when given money, would go to the newsstand to buy a paper. His friend insisted on a demonstration and handed the dog some money. The dog trotted off, but an hour later he had still not returned with the paper.

"How much did you give him?" asked the owner.

"Five dollars."

"Well, that explains it. When you give him five dollars he goes to the movies."

A woman had a dog who ran away every time he was let out of the house, and no matter how sweetly or how long she called his name, he wouldn't come home until he was good and ready. She sought advice at the pet shop.

"Well," said the salesman, "the best thing would be our new supersonic dog whistle. It's expensive, but well worth it in this case."

"Will my dog like the whistle?" the woman asked.

"Your dog will not only like the whistle," the salesman said, "but because of its design, your dog will be the only living thing to hear it. The only other living thing ever to respond to a whistle of this type was a big, dumb gorilla."

The woman was pleased, purchased the whistle and went home. That evening, as her husband watched TV, she opened the back door after the dog had been gone for ten minutes and blew the whistle as hard as she could.

"Who's blowing a whistle at this time of night?" demanded her husband.

—ALEX THIEN

"Why don't you go outside and chase a real car?"

❤ ❤ ❤ ❤ ❤ ❤ ❤ ❤ ❤ ❤ ❤

After our dog died, my parents had her cremated,
and they placed the ashes in a special box on
the fireplace mantel. One day the boy next door
came over to play and noticed the fancy container.
"What's in the box?" he asked.

"That's our dog," my mom replied.

"Oh," the boy simply said.

A minute later he remarked,

"He's awfully quiet, isn't he?"

—JOHN FERENCE

Two tourists notice a funeral procession with hordes of
men following a coffin led by a man and a vicious-looking dog.

The tourists stop the man at the front of the procession to
ask how the deceased died.

"This vicious dog attacked my mother-in-law," the man
replies.

The male tourist says, "May I borrow this dog?"

The man points to the crowd of men behind him and says,
"Wait your turn."

—JENNIFER READING

❤ ❤ ❤ ❤ ❤ ❤ ❤ ❤ ❤ ❤

The designer label craze has us all familiar with names. At a pet store I saw two dog sweaters labeled Pierre Cardog and Goochie Poochie.

—ELIYA OBILLO

The great thing about bumper stickers is they give proud parents a chance to boast about their children. The driver of the pickup in front of me was no different. His bumper sticker crowed "My Australian Cattle Dog Is Smarter Than Your Honor Student."

—STEWART BEUCKER

Each morning at 5:30, I take my Lhasa apso, Maxwell, for a walk. He has the bad habit of picking up bits of paper or other trash along the way. When he does, I command him to drop it, and he usually complies.

One morning, though, he absolutely refused to drop a piece of litter. So I told him to sit and then approached him to see what his treasure was. It was a $10 bill.

—ELSA BOGGS

I always scoffed when my sister insisted that our three dogs are computer literate. Then one day when I was signing on to AOL, I noticed that when the welcome voice came on, the dogs immediately settled down. **Later, when they heard the good-bye sign-off, all three dogs rushed to the door expecting to be walked.**

—MARGUERITE CANTINE

My neighbor's son picked up a stray dog and named it Sam. Sometime later, I was having coffee at their house and inquired about Sam.

"Oh, the dog is fine," my neighbor said. "She had a litter of puppies, and so we fixed the problem. Now we call her Sam Spayed."

—JUDY CHRISTENSEN

"Worst dog ever. Free to a good home. Not fixed. Doesn't come when called. Runs away. Kills chickens and has foul smell."

—LAURA CALENTINE, ATHENS (OHIO) NEWS

My three-year-old granddaughter was staying with me and proudly announced that she had brushed her teeth and then the dog's. The next day I bought her a new toothbrush.

"Why did you buy me this?" she asked.

"Because you brushed the dog's teeth with the old one," I told her.

"No I didn't, Nana," she said. "I used yours."

—BARBARA ROSE

The animal control center in my friend's town decided to conduct a dog census. A census taker called at my friend's home and, upon learning that she did indeed have a dog, asked what kind. "A brown dog," she replied.

"No, no. I mean what breed is the dog?"

"Well, I don't know, she's just a brown dog."

"Perhaps if I could see her," the man said, "I might be able to tell."

My friend brought out the dog and waited patiently while the man studied her pet. In the end, he noted on his form: "one brown dog."

—LEE WEAVER

♥ ♥ ♥ ♥ ♥ ♥ ♥ ♥ ♥ ♥ ♥

I needed help training my rambunctious dog.
So I decided to sign him up for some obedience classes.
Flipping through a catalog, I found one class that seemed
perfectly suited for my pup. The description read
"Dog Obedience, Monday; weeks: 8; Instructor: Catt."

—ANN MCKENRICK

George's friend Sam had a dog who could recite the
Gettysburg Address.
"Let me buy him from you," pleaded George after a
demonstration.
"Okay," agreed Sam. "All he knows is that Lincoln speech
anyway."
At his company's Fourth of July picnic, George brought his
new pet and announced that the animal could recite the entire
Gettysburg Address. No one believed him, and they proceeded
to place bets against the dog. George quieted the crowd and said,
"Now we'll begin!" Then he looked at the dog. The dog looked
back. No sound.
"Come on boy, do your stuff."
Nothing. A disappointed George took his dog and went
home.
"Why did you embarrass me like that in front of everybody?"
George yelled at the dog, "Do you realize how much money you
lost me?"
"Don't be silly, George," replied the dog, "think how much
you'll get at the Labor Day picnic if you treat me right."

—JOHN HUEHNERGARTH

♥ ♥ ♥ ♥ ♥ ♥ ♥ ♥ ♥ ♥ ♥

I was leaving the groomer's with my dog when I noticed a pet perfume in a display case. It's a wonder that we don't bowl each other over trying to get it, because the tagline boldly announced, "Strong enough for a man...but made for a chihuahua."

—BECKY KELLEY

Why Dogs Are Better Than Kids

- It doesn't take 45 minutes to get a dog ready to go outside in the winter.
- Dogs cannot lie.
- Dogs never resist nap time.
- You don't need to get extra phone lines for a dog.
- Dogs don't pester you about getting a kid.
- Dogs don't care if the peas have been touched by the mashed potatoes.
- Average cost of sending a dog to school: $42. Average cost of sending your kid: $103,000.
- Dogs are housebroken by the time they are 12 weeks old.
- Your dog is not embarrassed if you sing in public.
- If your dog is a bad seed, your genes cannot be blamed.

—JENNIFER BERMANN, *WHY DOGS ARE BETTER THAN KIDS* (ANDREWS MCMEEL)

Why did the cowboy buy a dachshund?
Someone told him to get a long little doggy.

❤ ❤ ❤ ❤ ❤ ❤ ❤ ❤ ❤ ❤ ❤

I saw two dogs walk over to a parking meter. One said to the other, **"How do you like that? Pay toilets."**

—DAVE STARR

For years, my family has kept a stray dog as our pet. One day, when my dad's friend came to visit, he asked my sister, "What is that mangy dog doing here?"

Offended, my sister replied, "He's our pet dog and he's like a member of the family."

Surprised, my dad's friend then asked, "Oh! Which one?"

—TAN PEI HONG

I put this question to my dog, a pet who puts on airs: "What, may I ask, makes man's best friend think he owns man's best chair?"

—DICK EMMONS

What Do You Get When You Cross...

...a collie and a Lhasa apso? A collapso, a dog that folds for easy transportation.

...a Pointer and a Setter? A Poinsetter, a traditional Christmas pet.

—ROSE C. WILSON FROM *PETS FOR LIFE*

I had always felt that my friend Neil's English bulldog was not the prettiest dog in the world. My suspicions were confirmed when one day we were taking Blue for a walk. A young boy approached and shyly asked Neil, "Mister, can I pet your pig?

—PAUL SCHNEIDER

♥ ♥ ♥ ♥ ♥ ♥ ♥ ♥ ♥ ♥ ♥

Who Wears the Collar in the Family?

New York City has many dogs, and it's not uncommon to hear people barking commands like, "Sit!" or "No!" or even "Don't sniff that!"

But Chris Atkins was taken aback when, as the light changed and a number of pedestrians started to cross the street, a man said to his dog: "Okay, Max, let's go. And please, let's not forget what almost happened the last time."

—THE NEW YORK TIMES

"When did you start seeing the invisible fence?"

♥ ♥ ♥ ♥ ♥ ♥ ♥ ♥ ♥ ♥ ♥

My sister, her husband and their English springer spaniel dog, Sam, stopped at a garage one day when their car horn wouldn't work. Dave slipped out of the driver's seat and the mechanic slid in to check the horn. From the back seat, Sam gently pressed his nose to the man's ear and sniffed. The mechanic screamed and almost fell to the ground in his haste to escape from the car. "I thought your wife was trying to kiss me," he explained later.

—ANNE CROCKER

A man walks into a wine bar with his dog.

"Er, excuse me," says the barman. "No dogs allowed."

"It's okay," the man responds. "This is a super-intelligent, talking dog."

"Oh, yeah?" sneers the barman. "Prove it."

"What grows on trees?" the man asks the animal.

"Bark, bark," replies the dog.

"What do you find on top of a house?"

"Roof, roof," says the mutt.

"What's the opposite of smooth?"

"Rough, rough," growls the hound.

The barman realizes he's being made a fool of and throws the man and his dog out.

"Well, I'm terribly sorry about that, Gavin," says the dog to his owner outside on the pavement. "Just out of interest, which one did I get wrong?"

♥ ♥ ♥ ♥ ♥ ♥ ♥ ♥ ♥ ♥ ♥

Notice in pet shop window: **Five puppies, FREE. Mother a crossbred Labrador. Father a small brown and white dog capable of climbing six-foot fence.**

—MRS. CHRIS SCOTT

During the Friday evening service, a rabbi notices Bernie, a congregation member, walk in with a Rottweiler. Horrified, the rabbi rushes over.

"What are you doing in here with that dog?" he asks Bernie. "It's deeply inappropriate."

"He's here to worship."

"Pull the other one," says the rabbi.

"I'm telling the truth!" protests Bernie and nods to the dog. It produces a yarmulke and tallith and puts them on. Then it opens a prayer book and starts praying in Hebrew.

The rabbi listens rapt for 15 minutes and is deeply impressed by the quality of the praying. "Sorry to have doubted you," he says. "Do you think your dog would consider going to rabbinical school?"

Bernie, throws up his arms in disgust. "You talk to him," he says. "He wants to be a doctor!"

Our much loved elderly dog had to go for a long delayed grooming session and I warned the staff that Sam is now deaf. "To get some response from him and get his attention," I advised them, "make eye contact and use hand signals."

The girl assistant asked, "So what's new? Isn't that what you have to do with all males?" I knew Sam was in safe hands.

—GLORIA O'DONNELL

Cunning
cats

Cats are intended to
teach us that not
everything in nature has
a purpose.

—GARRISON KEILLOR

♥ ♥ ♥ ♥ ♥ ♥ ♥ ♥ ♥ ♥ ♥

"Reward! Lost black male cat (Chucky).
May have gotten into vehicle & driven to other area."

—MARY ANN JOHNSTON

When I hired my part-time housekeeper, I made it clear that her duties did not extend to feeding the cat, since that was the responsibility of my children. Whiskers, however, was not aware of our arrangement.

One day he was being particularly persistent in his demands to be fed. My housekeeper, with her hands on her hips, looked down at him and said sternly, "I don't do cats."

—BARBARA BEAHM

Johnny's mother stops to watch her son read the Bible to their cat. "Isn't that sweet?" she says. But an hour later she hears a terrible racket. Running out the door, she finds Johnny stuffing the cat into a bucket of water.

"Johnny, what are you doing?"

"I'm baptizing Muffin," he replies.

"But cats don't like to be in water."

"Well then, he shouldn't have joined my church."

Every morning my son and daughter-in-law's cat would sit just outside their bedroom patio doors at daybreak demanding to be let in. To break the cat of this annoying habit, one night they put a bucket of water in their room ready for the morning. When the cat started its persistent yowling, my son, half asleep, leaped out of bed, grabbed the bucket and threw the water at the cat. The patio doors were closed.

—THELMA JOHNSON

I was waitressing in a restaurant where the owner's black cat was notorious for sneaking in to enjoy the warmth of the open fire. One night as a couple were dining by candlelight near the fire, I noticed a black object under the woman's chair.

I reached down as discreetly as possible to grab what I thought was our recalcitrant cat when the woman asked indignantly, "What on earth are you doing with my handbag?"

—MARINDA HAWTHORNE

♥ ♥ ♥ ♥ ♥ ♥ ♥ ♥ ♥ ♥ ♥

I worked at a boarding kennel where people leave their dogs and cats while on vacation. One morning I had taken a cat out of his cage, and after playing with him and replenishing his food and water, I put him back in. A few minutes later, I was surprised to see the feline at my feet, since the cage doors lock automatically when they're shut. I couldn't figure out how the cat escaped, until I bent down to pick him up and spied his name tag: Houdini.

—BARBARA ROHRSSEN

When John's cat, Willie, got stuck in a tree, we told John not to worry.

"He'll come down when he gets good and hungry," we said.

Three days later, with Willie still up in the tree, John could stand it no longer and climbed after him. The man was 60 feet up when the cat scampered to the ground.

"It's all right, John, you can come down now," we shouted. Total silence, and then the fearful reply: "I'll come down when I'm good and hungry."

—NINA HARTNETT

While I was waiting my turn at the veterinarian's office, a woman came in holding a large cat.

"Do you really want to have Mitzie de-clawed?" asked the receptionist.

"Shhhh!" the woman said as she hastily covered her cat's ears, **"I told her she was coming in for a manicure."**

—LUANNE BERGSTROM

♥ ♥ ♥ ♥ ♥ ♥ ♥ ♥ ♥ ♥ ♥

After we moved to the country, our cat, Sadie, became a particularly good mouser. I praised her efforts, and she began leaving the mice in conspicuous places so my husband could dispose of them. Along the way, Sadie even developed a good understanding of men. One morning, courtesy of Sadie, my husband found a dead mouse lying on the sofa next to the television remote control.

—BARBARA DIANNIBELLA

Licorice, our cat, usually misses when she tries to pounce on birds. Occasionally, she gets lucky and dashes into the bushes with her prize. If I see this happen, I take my seven-iron and beat the bushes, frightening the cat so the bird can fly to safety. Once, I was whacking the shrubbery with my golf club and shouting, "Get out! Get out of there now!" when a man on the patio next door spoke up.

"Why not just take the two-stroke penalty?"

—KEN KRIVANEK

As a chaplain in a university residence hall, I am supposed to uphold all of the school rules, which include a ban on pets. That changed, however, when a kitten adopted me. The freshmen in my dorm kept my secret. They covered for me by calling my kitten the Book, since I had so many in my room. One morning I was leaving the dorm with the kitten in a carrier. A student stopped me and asked, "Where are you taking the Book?" I explained that I was bringing the kitten to the vet. "She's getting neutered today," I told him. "Hmm," the student responded, "no sequels."

—TOM POWERS

**"I hope you're not allergic to cats—
I'd hate to see you go."**

One woman in our tour group was a strict vegetarian. When she talked about her cat, though, she admitted that she fed her pampered pet expensive canned meats.

"Why is it all right for your cat to eat meat if it isn't for you?" I finally asked her.

"My cat and I don't have the same beliefs," she replied.

—DORA GIGGY

**Which animal do you think is clever—
a cat or a dog?**

A cat, of course. Have you ever seen cats
pulling sleds through snow and ice?

— ANATOLY FROLOV

The first-grade children in a Raleigh, N.C., school were having a wonderful time playing with a stray cat. After a while one little lad asked the teacher if it was a boy cat or a girl cat. Not wishing to get into that particular subject, she said that she didn't believe she could tell.

"I know how we can find out," said the boy.

"All right," said the teacher, resigning herself to the inevitable, "how can we find out?"

"We can vote," said the child.

—SAM RAGAN

Our neighbor asked my granddaughter what she put on her cat to make him smell so good.

"Maybe it's the perfume I use," came the reply. "The cat sleeps with his nose against my neck, so some of the scent must rub off on him."

The next evening our neighbor was in a department store when she noticed a familiar fragrance in the air. She asked the woman who had just walked by what perfume she was wearing. After learning the name, our neighbor said, over the heads of all in the crowded store, "It smells wonderful. My friend's cat wears it."

—T. ELLSWORTH CLARK

♥ ♥ ♥ ♥ ♥ ♥ ♥ ♥ ♥ ♥ ♥

A dog doesn't want much and is happy to get it.
A cat doesn't know what it wants and wants
more of it.

—RICHARD HEXEM

A Seattle woman was in the midst of preparations for a dinner for 16 when Penelope, a neighbor's cat, wandered in and kept getting underfoot. Annoyed, the hostess finally burst out, "Oh, go catch a mouse!" and shooed the cat out of the house.

The dinner was a success, and the guests were contentedly sipping their coffee when Penelope appeared in a dining room window, leaped lightly to the table and carefully placed a dead mouse beside the hostess' cup.

As I left the house to go to a luncheon party, one of my husband's students from the hostel house up the street came running toward me.

"Come quickly!" he shouted.

Fearing that one of the boys was in trouble, I took off after him, hanging on desperately to my fancy hat. We dashed into the house and upstairs, and there in the middle of a bed the fraternity cat was having kittens. The boys were all standing around solicitously, and a pre-medical student appeared to have the situation well in hand.

"What do you want me to do, John?" I asked after I caught my breath.

"Why, we don't want you to do anything, ma'am," he said, looking surprised. "We just thought there ought to be a lady present."

—ANONYMOUS

QUOTABLE QUOTES

"The cat could very well be man's best friend but would never stoop to admitting it."

—DOUG LARSON

"You cannot look at a sleeping cat and feel tense."

—JANE PAULEY

"The problem with cats is that they get the exact same look on their face whether they see a moth or an axe murderer."

—PAULA POUNDSTONE

"There's no dealing with a cat who knows you're awake."

—BRAD SOLOMON

"The only mystery about the cat is why it ever decided to become a domestic animal."

—COMPTON MACKENZIE

"Does it ever amaze and delight you that of all the places in the world— cold grassy nests under hedgerows, warm patches of sun on a carpet—the cat chooses to sit on your lap?"

—NEVADA BARR, *SEEKING ENLIGHTENMENT* (PUTNAM)

"When I play with my cat, who knows if I am not more of a pastime to her than she is to me?"

—MONTAIGNE

"The interesting thing about being a mother is that everyone wants pets, but no one but me cleans the kitty litter."

—MERYL STREEP IN *VOGUE*

♥ ♥ ♥ ♥ ♥ ♥ ♥ ♥ ♥ ♥ ♥

In the crowded suburban bus, the voice of a six-year-old returning homeward with his mother after a day of shopping, rang out loud and clear, "Is our cat a daddy cat or a mother cat?"

"He's a daddy cat," the mother replied patiently.

"How do we know he's a daddy cat?" the boy asked.

An expectant hush fell over the bus, and the passengers listened attentively to see how the mother would handle this one. She was ready for the challenge.

"He's got whiskers, hasn't he?" she said.

—JOE McCARTHY

My 18-year-old daughter and I were sitting in the yard one afternoon when our cat sauntered by.

"That cat certainly has a great life," I remarked. "She comes and goes just as she darn well pleases."

"That," my daughter replied dryly, "is because she doesn't live with her mother."

—NANCY SIEGEL

"What would you like?" my wife asked as she prepared the evening meal. "Tuna, salmon, chicken, beef or liver?"

Surprised and pleased by this unusual opportunity to make a selection from such an extensive dinner menu, I replied, "Beef would be nice for a change, thank you."

"Oh," she said, **"I wasn't talking to you. I was asking the cat. We're having soup."**

—C. REDDEN

❤ ❤ ❤ ❤ ❤ ❤ ❤ ❤ ❤ ❤ ❤

Notice seen in London:
Found: Tabby kitten with white paws and bib.
Very affectionate. Answers to the name Go Away.

While at a friend's house, I told him to keep his small son at least five feet from the color television because radiation from the set might cause sterility.

"Really?" exclaimed my friend, and he plumped the family cat in front of the set.

—B. D. WILDMAN

Delivering a registered letter on my postal round, I rang the doorbell of the address but no one answered. Instead a cat appeared and settled by the door.

I delivered the post to the upstairs flat and then went back down to the front to post the registered letter card.

When I arrived, I found the occupant at his door looking rather distressed. "Am I glad to see you," he said. "I thought our cat had learned how to ring the doorbell."

DAVID CROSS

LOST, screamed the ad in *The Daily Standard* of Celina, Ohio. Female medium-size gray tiger cat. Answers to Lucy or Here Kitty, Kitty, Kitty.

—RICHARD FLAUGHER

"They say that a black cat brings bad luck. Is that true?"
"Depends on who comes across it: a human, or a mouse."

—CHAYAN

♥ ♥ ♥ ♥ ♥ ♥ ♥ ♥ ♥ ♥ ♥

My friend Nancy's babysitter confronted her about the new kitten. "That cat of yours is going to destroy your furniture in no time!" she exclaimed.

A smile grew on Nancy's face. "That's the plan," she said.

—KITTY COCHRANE

Our young daughter had adopted a stray cat. To my distress, he began to use the back of our new sofa as a scratching post.

"Don't worry," my husband reassured me, "I'll have him trained in no time."

I watched for several days as my husband patiently "trained" our new pet. Whenever the cat scratched, my husband deposited him outdoors to teach him a lesson. The cat learned quickly. For the next 16 years, whenever he wanted to go outside, he scratched the back of the sofa.

—LISA GOLDRICK

When our cat had her third litter, we were hard-pressed to find willing owners for the kittens. We decided to leave them in a basket on the front porch of a good-natured friend of ours who was celebrating his birthday.

We put the basket on his doorstep with a note attached: "To Fred on his birthday, many little joyous greetings." Later, our doorbell rang. On our porch was the basket of kittens, with a new note: **"Many happy returns."**

—BETTY L. AERICK

QUOTABLE QUOTES

"Women and cats will do as they please, and men and dogs should relax and get used to the idea."

—ROBERT A. HEINLEIN

To a cat, "NO!" means "Not while I'm looking." —UNKNOWN

"Cats are notoriously sore losers. Coming in second best, especially to someone as poorly coordinated as a human being, grates their sensibility."

—STEPHEN BAKER

"Every dog has his day—but the nights are reserved for the cats."

—UNKNOWN

"Cats names are more for human benefit. They give one a certain degree of confidence that the animal belongs to you. "

—ALAN AYCKBOURN *TABLE MANNERS*

"No matter how much cats fight, there always seems to be plenty of kittens."

—ABRAHAM LINCOLN

"Thousands of years ago, cats were worshipped as gods. Cats have never forgotten this."

—ANONYMOUS

"Cat: A pygmy lion who loves mice, hates dogs and patronizes human beings."

—OLIVER HERFORD

♥ ♥ ♥ ♥ ♥ ♥ ♥ ♥ ♥ ♥ ♥

Our neighbor's cat was run over by a car, and the mother quickly disposed of the remains before her four-year-old son, Billy, found out about it. After a few days, though, Billy finally asked about the cat.

"Billy, the cat died," his mother explained. "But it's all right. He's up in heaven with God."

The boy asked, **"What in the world would God want with a dead cat?"**

—ROSS SAMS, JR.

My friend Kelly's cat, Sam, loved riding in Kelly's car, and it was always a battle if the cat was outside and he wanted to leave it at home. One day Kelly left Sam on the front steps and got into his car. He was on the highway when suddenly he had to slam on the brakes to avoid the car ahead, and a screaming ball of fur slid down the front windshield. Afterward, Sam travelled everywhere with Kelly.

—TERRI-LYNN ROEMER

Every year, we go on vacation to the same place, and our old cat comes with us. The butcher we buy our meat from knows him well now. One day, when I was picking up an order, I asked him, "Would you have any old scraps of meat?"

"Aha," he said, "is it for the old fellow? Isn't he dead yet?"

"He doesn't seem to be," I replied.

I paid and turned around to leave the store only to catch the horrified looks of two customers who were waiting to be served.

—CHRISTIANE MORLET

❝Regarding the furniture, I blame the catnip
and I'm entering rehab.❞

❤ ❤ ❤ ❤ ❤ ❤ ❤ ❤ ❤ ❤ ❤

One day I stopped by to visit my friend, the mother of two teenage daughters. Through the screen door I was aghast to hear her say: "I've really had it with you two and your boyfriends! As soon as I get the money, I'm getting you both fixed!"

I was greatly relieved to find out she was talking to her dog, nursing eight puppies, and to her very pregnant cat.

—M. J. MCCOLL

From a neighbor who had gone to Maine
for a week's vacation, a woman in Melrose, Mass.,
received a postcard which bore
this message:

"Would you please feed my cat while I'm away?
She will eat anything,
but don't put yourself out."

—JOHN J. MCALEER

Living in a household with eight indoor cats requires buying large amounts of kitty litter, which I usually get in 25-pound bags—100 pounds at a time. When I was going to be out of town for a week, I decided to go to the supermarket to stock up.

As my husband and I both pushed shopping carts, each loaded with five large bags of litter, a man looked at our purchases and queried, "Bengal or Siberian?"

—JUDY J. HAGG

♥ ♥ ♥ ♥ ♥ ♥ ♥ ♥ ♥ ♥

I was waiting in line at my county clerk's office one afternoon and noticed a hand-lettered sign that read: **Any child left unattended will be given a free kitten.**

—JEANNE MAULTSKY

Five Signs Your Cat is Plotting to Kill You
- Seems mighty chummy with the dog all of a sudden.
- Unexplained calls to F. Lee Bailey's 900 number on your bill.
- Ball of yarn tied playfully into a hangman's noose.
- Droppings in litter box spell out "REDRUM."
- You find a piece of paper labeled "My Wil" which reads, "Leev awl kat."

—DAVID BROOME

A gnome is in the garden busily destroying some bushes when a house cat appears. "What are you?" asks the cat.

"A gnome," comes the reply. "I steal food from humans, I kill their plants, I make annoying music at night to drive them crazy, and I love mischief. And what, may I ask, are you?"

The cat replies, "Um, I'm a gnome."

—BLAKE KILTOFF

My brother and his roommate once smuggled two kittens into their college dormitory room. The felines' favorite place to catnap was in the letter trays, so the animals were dubbed **In and Out.**

—SYLVIA L. MAYE

♥ ♥ ♥ ♥ ♥ ♥ ♥ ♥ ♥ ♥ ♥

The vet prescribed daily tablets for our geriatric cat, Tigger, and after several battles my husband devised a way to give her the medication. It involved wrapping Tigger in a towel, trapping her between his knees, forcing her mouth open and depositing the pill on the back of her tongue.

David was proud of his resourcefulness until one hectic session when he lost control of both cat and medicine. Tigger leaped out of his grasp, paused to inspect the tablet—which had rolled across the floor—and then ate it.

—MADI LEGERE

My marriage brought with it four adult stepchildren (only one of whom I met before the wedding) and a cat. Soon after our honeymoon, my husband and I invited the children to our apartment for a get-to-know-you dinner. I was nervous and wanted to impress the kids with my ability to take care of their father and his cat. The apartment was neat and tidy, and I had cooked a lovely dinner. We greeted the kids with hugs, but they paid as much attention to the cat as to me. Wanting them to know my regard for the cat, I blurted out, "I've never lived with an animal before I married your father."

—JENNIFER GAUCI

Our gas and electric company servicemen are used to finding notes from customers advising them about various pets to be encountered in the house. But a recent one caused our man to do a double take—and this was all he took. The note said: Furnace is in hallway—do service. Dogs are in kitchen—do avoid. Guinea pig in hallway—do not squash. Cats everywhere—do take one home.

♥ ♥ ♥ ♥ ♥ ♥ ♥ ♥ ♥ ♥ ♥

A cat sits on a bench next to a miserable-looking college student. The young man notices that the cat is looking up at him, so he takes the opportunity to unburden himself of his troubles.

"I've spent every dime I had saved, maxed out my credit cards and can't get another student loan.

"I can't pay for school, can't even afford to take a girl out for a drink. What could be worse than being young and broke?"

Says the cat, "Try being young and fixed."

When we moved with our cat to Melfort, Sask., the neighbors soon informed us that they weren't cat people. That was fine: We knew where we stood.

About two months after the move, our neighbor called. "Don't you know your cat has been sitting outside in the cold waiting for you for 20 minutes?" she scolded.

Less than a month later, she called again. "What's wrong with our cat?" she worried. "I bought her steak and she won't eat it."

That's when I realized our cat had two homes and double meals.

—OLGA MCKELLAR

When my daughter and I caught only one perch on our fishing trip—not enough for even a modest lunch—we decided to feed it to her two cats. She put our catch in their dish and watched as the two pampered pets sniffed at the fish but refused to eat it.

Thinking quickly, my daughter then picked up the dish, walked over to the electric can opener, ran it for a few seconds, then put the fish back down. The cats dug right in.

—SUSAN WARD

"Look Whiskers, I think this violates the doctor/patient relationship."

♥ ♥ ♥ ♥ ♥ ♥ ♥ ♥ ♥ ♥

During the night, strange noises don't usually concern me as my cat, Benny, frequently plays toss and chase with his toy mouse in the middle of the night. This time though, the sound that had woken me was more of a thumping and banging. I lay there listening for a few moments, then I heard the noise right in my bedroom! I bravely reached over and turned on the light and saw Benny with his head stuck in an empty tissue box.

—WILMA HAMER

Husband, as wife shows him cat surrounded by new kittens: "She did all right for a cat that didn't know a soul in the neighborhood three months ago."

—BOB BARNES

The seniors' facility where I work has a resident cat named Frank. At the front door of the building there's a keypad; to exit, you must enter the correct sequence of numbers. One day, a visitor noticed Frank at his feet just as he was about to leave and he turned to a nearby senior and asked, "Is the cat allowed out?"

"Oh yes," she told him smiling. "He just hasn't learned the numbers yet?

—J. FERGUSON

Late one night I heard our cat running back and forth in our bedroom, batting at something on the floor on my husband's side of the bed. I woke my husband and asked him if the cat was playing with a mouse. A half-asleep and confused reply came from his side of the bed, **"You mean on the computer?"**

❤ ❤ ❤ ❤ ❤ ❤ ❤ ❤ ❤ ❤ ❤

My parents were preparing to leave for Nova Scotia
for a holiday and I was to take care of their cat,
Mittens, while they were away. In order to
cut costs, my mom told me that she'd only call me
in an emergency.

Two weeks later, I was feeding the cat when
the phone rang. The cat ran to the phone, and when
the answering machine clicked on, I heard my
mother talking to Mittens. As she said goodbye she
promised to call again that night.

Curious, I checked the answering machine and saw that

Mom had made 28 calls to Mittens in the two weeks since they'd been gone!

—ROB DUNSWORTH

After house hunting for many months, my husband and I
finally found the home we wanted to buy. Our young sons voiced
their approval. When I asked what they liked best about it, my
four-year-old answered, "The goldfish and the cat."

—JUDY REYNO

“And to think he was so cute and tiny when he was a kitten!”

♥ ♥ ♥ ♥ ♥ ♥ ♥ ♥ ♥ ♥ ♥

Just how much our cat, Judi, is treated like a member of the family became apparent the day we took her to the vet. I was filling out her medical form when my husband, looking over my shoulder, exclaimed, "I didn't know she spelled her name like that!"

—SELINE KUTAN

On a cold winter day, my six-year-old daughter, Elise, was cuddling our Burmese cat in a chair by the fire. As the cat purred contentedly, Elise said, "Look, Mom, he really loves me."

I smiled and said, "He has good taste." There was a brief silence followed by, "You're right, Mom. He does taste good."

—JILL MILNER

One night while I was cat-sitting my daughter's indoor feline, it escaped outside. When it failed to return the following morning, I found the beast clinging to a branch about 30 feet up in a spindly tree. Unable to lure it down, I called the fire department.

"We don't do that anymore," the woman dispatcher said. When I persisted, she was polite but firm. "The cat will come down when it gets hungry enough."

"How do you know that?" I asked.

"Have you ever seen a cat skeleton in a tree?" she said.

Two hours later the cat was back, looking for breakfast.

—TERRY CHRISTIANSEN

 What's a cat's favorite dessert?
Chocolate mousse.

—AMITA MANI

❤ ❤ ❤ ❤ ❤ ❤ ❤ ❤ ❤ ❤ ❤

Bartender to customer as they watch a cat eat from a bowl on the bar: "It's okay, those are kitty treats anyway."

—WILMA HAMER, VERNON

I was tired and had just reached that almost-asleep moment when my teenage daughter let out a terrifying wail. Our normally placid cat had caught a mouse and both were under her bed. This woke her roommate who added to the din.

Realizing I had to do something before the neighbors complained, I called my son away from his usual position in front of the TV and told him it was his problem: his sister, his girlfriend and his cat. He dealt with it promptly by sending in his dog.

—CHERYL BURNS

My three young children had been asking my husband and me for a pet since they were old enough to talk. Being so busy, the last thing we wanted was more responsibility added to our schedules, so we attempted to fill their pet needs with battery-operated animals. But still they begged for a real pet.

Finally, I gave in and brought home a little orange tabby, then waited for the kids to arrive home from school.

Excited, my five-year-old son, Jesse, examined the kitten for a few minutes, then asked, "Can I call Grandma to tell her about our new cat?"

I agreed and dialed my mother's number. "Grandma, Grandma, we got a cat!" Jesse exclaimed. "A real cat! It doesn't even have any batteries."

—SYLVIE BÉLANGER

♥ ♥ ♥ ♥ ♥ ♥ ♥ ♥ ♥ ♥ ♥

While an old lady is polishing an antique lamp, a genie appears and gives her three wishes. She asks to be young and rich and for her cat to turn into a handsome prince.

Her wishes granted, the prince takes the lady in his arms. As long-forgotten feelings stir, the prince whispers to her, **"Now, I bet you're sorry you took me to the vet for that little operation."**

—SUSAN CARR

A man who lived next door to a pub had a favorite tabby cat. Unfortunately the cat was run over by a car and killed. A year later, at about midnight, the pub owner was doing his accounts. Suddenly the ghost of this cat appeared in front of him, holding half his tail in his paw.

"Can you help me, please?" said the cat's ghost. "I expect you remember me when I lived next door. My old master has moved, so I thought I would try you."

"Yes, I do remember you," said the pub owner. "You were a nice cat. What can I do for you?"

"Well," said the cat's ghost. "You see this bit of tail that I'm holding in my hand? It was cut off in my accident and I'm fed up carrying it around with me. Can you mend it for me, please?"

"I'm sorry," said the owner, "but much as I would like to, I can't help you. I'm not allowed to retail spirits after eleven o'clock."

—BRIAN JOHNSTON

♥ ♥ ♥ ♥ ♥ ♥ ♥ ♥ ♥ ♥ ♥

Before I rush out to work, I give my hair a quick going over with a brush I leave on the hall table. One morning I was horrified to see my son grooming the cat with my hairbrush. "What do you think you're doing?" I demanded.

He looked puzzled and said, "But I do this every day."

—BONNIE GAUTHIER

Our curious kitten Bandit tried to open the glass shower doors every time I was behind them. One morning my husband, Chad, lifted Bandit so he could see over the doors while I was showering. "See," I heard Chad say as the kitten peered down at me, "there's nothing exciting in there."

—BETH CANTRELL

I was diagnosed with hypothyroidism some years ago, then we learned that our 12-year-old cat had the same condition. When my 36-year-old daughter thought she might have some of the symptoms, she suggested to her doctor that perhaps she should have a blood test to check it out. He asked if anyone in her family had a thyroid gland disorder. "Yes," she answered, "my father and the cat."

—FRANK J. KENNEDY

Isn't it unfair that women love cats? Cats are independent, they don't listen, they don't come when you call, they like to stay out all night and when they are at home they like to be left alone to sleep.

In other words, every quality that women hate in a man, they love in a cat.

—TERRY SANGSTER

"In retrospect, I could have done more with my lives."

♥ ♥ ♥ ♥ ♥ ♥ ♥ ♥ ♥ ♥ ♥

Having acquired a stray kitten, we bought him a little collar with his name and telephone number on it. We didn't see much of Sidney. He was always off somewhere getting into mischief. Soon I began to get irate calls from my neighbors.

"Are you Sidney's mother? He's just eaten my goldfish!"

"Your cat's terrorizing my Yorkshire terrier!"

"Have you got a cat named Sidney? He's just knocked a dozen eggs off the table!"

Tired of apologizing, I asked a friend, who was good with cats, what to do. The solution was simple: "Take his collar off."

—ANN CROOKS

When my six-year-old grandson heard that my cat had died, he asked where the cat was now. I told him Grandpa had buried him in the garden. As the son of two avid gardeners, he then asked, "Will another one grow?"

—F. BAKER

My daughter, Lucy, adopted an old abandoned cat that insisted on eating its meals outside the back door, and only at night. Because of his advanced age, Lucy called him Grandpa.

Imagine the horror of her dinner guests one evening when she scraped the leftovers onto a plate and announced,

"These are for Grandpa. He's waiting on the back steps."

—GILLIAN YUNG

♥ ♥ ♥ ♥ ♥ ♥ ♥ ♥ ♥ ♥ ♥

**Free: One owner, low-mileage used cat.
Answers to Tabitha or electric can opener.**

Niggy, our pampered black cat, was never late for his evening meal, so we were worried when he didn't turn up one wet evening. Our search in the murky darkness ended when we spotted him with its head jammed in the access hole of our garden incinerator lid and some fur lost while trying to free himself.

All efforts by us and neighbors failed to free the cat, and the local veterinarian fared no better. Finally, we turned to the fire department, who used their "jaws of life" to cut through the lid. The instant they freed the cat, it bolted into the darkness.

The next morning, Niggy showed up at our back door, unscathed and blissfully unaware that he had been mistaken for someone else's pet.

—M. PIPER

I was awakened at 4:30 a.m. by a loud, constant chirrup. After a while, annoyed, I slipped on my housecoat, headed to the door and switched on the outside lights. The singing stopped, so I turned off the lights, but seconds later it started again. I peered outside and met a pair of shining eyes glaring at me. The neighbor's cat was stalking our new garden ornament: a motion detector singing robin.

—J. K. RUTLEY

Mother: "Don't pull the cat's tail."
Daughter: "I didn't, Mom. I only held its tail, but it pulled my arm."

—PRINCESS SIRINDHORN

♥ ♥ ♥ ♥ ♥ ♥ ♥ ♥ ♥ ♥ ♥

 What do you call a cat that joins the Red Cross?

A first-aid kit.

AMITA MANI

My husband went to the cardiologist after experiencing symptoms of a heart attack.

"I had taken our cat to the vet," he told the nurse, "and while I was there, my chest got tight, and I had trouble breathing. Later, my left arm began aching."

The nurse was clearly concerned. "So," she asked, "how was the cat?"

—GAIL WEBSTER

On their way to town, a five-minute drive on the highway, my husband and three children wondered why other drivers were honking their horns. Upon arriving at a set of traffic lights, a lady in the next lane rolled down her window and yelled, "Your cat's on the roof!"

—PATTY MCKECHNIE

My cat's technicolor coat earned her the name of Fruit Salad. A loving creature, she's also a thief and has been the cause of many complaints. One afternoon I was confronted by a neighbor whose dinner had been stolen from the kitchen table. Wanting to positively identify the culprit, I asked, "Was it Fruit Salad?"

"No," she replied, "It was rump steak."

—MRS. E. LOMBARD

♥ ♥ ♥ ♥ ♥ ♥ ♥ ♥ ♥ ♥ ♥

When she realized one of her kittens was missing, my friend Toba optimistically posted a few notices around town. Within a week, Toba received a call from a woman with a kitten that matched the description. "You'd better hurry, though," she advised. "My son is getting pretty attached to it."

Wanting to ease the boy's unhappiness at returning the kitten, Toba picked up some fast-food coupons on the way to his house, as well as some cookies and balloons for him and discovered when she got there that the son was 35 years old.

—DARLENE HORN

My seven-year-old son, Josh, was playing in his room. "And our action-figure hero is menaced by a giant monster cat," he yelled, waving his toy in front of our cat, Ghost, who was obligingly playing his part in the drama and batting at the toy. "Then our hero jumps on the monster cat and throws him to the ground!"

Careful not to hurt his pet, Josh began patting the cat gently. Then, with a disgusted voice, he said, "Monsters don't purr!"

—DEANNA BATES

A motorist approached a neighbor one afternoon and said, "I'm awfully sorry, but I think I've just run over your cat. Can I replace it?"

 The neighbor looked the motorist up and down and said, **"I doubt if you'd be the mouser she was."**

—ANTHONY GRAHAM

♥ ♥ ♥ ♥ ♥ ♥ ♥ ♥ ♥ ♥ ♥

Overheard: "The best way to get my son out
of bed in the morning is to toss the cat on it.
He sleeps with the dog."

—MICHELLE BORTEN

Young Rodney was in the garden filling in a hole when
his neighbor peered over the fence and asked him what he was
doing.

"My goldfish died," replied little Rodney tearfully, "and I've
just buried him."

The neighbor was concerned: "That's an awfully large hole
for a goldfish, isn't it?"

Young Rodney patted down the heap of earth and answered,
"That's because he's inside your horrid cat."

One little girl in my wife's first-grade class appeared to be on
the verge of tears. Sherren took her aside and asked what was
wrong. "My mommy is allergic to my new kitten," the girl said.
"Oh, that's too bad," sympathized Sherren. "Will you have to
give her away?"

**"No," the child sobbed. "Daddy says
the kitty has to go."**

—ALFRED MORRISON

♥ ♥ ♥ ♥ ♥ ♥ ♥ ♥ ♥ ♥ ♥

My young cousin was playing outside one day when she was bitten by a cat. My aunt scooped her daughter up and raced inside to call the hospital. The nurse listened as she explained what had happened. "Are her shots up to date?" the nurse asked.

"I don't know," my frazzled aunt replied. "It was a stray cat."

—LORI UKRAINETZ

On arriving at my factory one morning, I found it had been burgled for the fourth time in seven months. When the police and chief security officer arrived to investigate, I asked what else I could do to protect the premises, as I already employed a guard. The security officer suggested I get a dog. "But we have a cat," I replied without thinking, worrying about the safety of the animal. "Ah," replied the security officer. "But it cannot bark."

—M. A. TORR

One evening, when our children were already sleeping and my husband was at work, I decided to pamper myself. To create a nice mood, I turned off lights, lit candles, had a bath with fragrant salts, made a cucumber mask for my face, and as I relaxed, I stretched on the couch. As soft music was playing, I sipped wine, filling my mind with soothing thoughts. In such a blissful state, I fell asleep.

Suddenly I woke up, and I saw a pair of green eyes in front me. I screamed. I jumped off the couch and turned on the light. It was my cat. Normally a gentle animal, this time his hair stood up and he was growling. It turned out that my cat, profiting from my sleep, decided to lick off the cucumber mask.

—IRENA KAMINSKA-PLACZEK

❤ ❤ ❤ ❤ ❤ ❤ ❤ ❤ ❤ ❤ ❤

My cat used to go to our neighbor's house and disturb him. One night the neighbor knocked at our door to complain. Being polite, he didn't want to be hasty in his judgment and make unnecessary trouble. In order to be sure he was accusing the right cat, he asked, in a formal tone, "Is your cat at home?"

—MARIA CAROLINA FALLEIROS

It may be said that on behalf of a recently developed robot cat that it needs no food, drink or litter box. Controlled by a microchip, it is capable of purring, crying when spoken to and rolling in various directions at the owner's hand clap. Call that a cat? Unless they can program it to come home with a half-chewed ear, drop a dead mouse at your feet and stalk contemptuously from the room, it's an imposter. If it does anything on human demand, it's no cat.

Our cat, Meowski, is a handsome black cat with white markings. He is also a very determined hunter. We put a bell on his collar to give the local wildlife a chance, only to discover he worked out how to remove it. Meowski doesn't tend to hunt the most endangered species; only sparrows, mice and the odd lizard, but it is still a concern of ours.

We came home one day to find beautiful blue feathers in the hallway. We immediately presumed the worst, suspecting that a rare native parrot had become his latest victim. We followed the trail of feathers to the bedroom, the place where he usually offers up his conquests. There it was under the bed: the remnants of a neighbor's feather duster.

—BRAD WALKER

♥ ♥ ♥ ♥ ♥ ♥ ♥ ♥ ♥ ♥ ♥

"I feel sorry for this soldier," joked my husband as he handed me a flier he'd found in our mailbox. It read:

Lost Cat
Black and white
Answers to Nat
Belongs to a soldier
Recently neutered

—SONDRA GILBERTSON

First cat: "How did you get on in the milk-drinking competition?"

Second cat: "Oh, I won by six laps."

—MARY NORMANTON

My friend's daughter, Chelsea, found a baby tooth that her kitten had lost. She and her sister decided that they could put one over on the tooth fairy. That night they placed the tooth under Chelsea's pillow. And it worked. But the tooth fairy left a can of sardines.

—SANDRA E. MARTIN

Tweety birds

A bird doesn't sing because
it has an answer;
it sings because it has a song.

—MAYA ANGELOU

♥ ♥ ♥ ♥ ♥ ♥ ♥ ♥ ♥ ♥ ♥

My wife desperately wanted a parrot. When she found one advertised in the paper, we went to meet it. The owner, however, admitted that the bird had one annoying habit. "He has learned to mimic the ear-piercing sound of the smoke alarm," he said.

"But don't worry. For some reason, he only repeats it when my wife is in the kitchen."

—BARRY G., CLASSIFIEDGUYS.COM

It was my first year teaching tenth-graders geometry, and I was frustrated with the lack of effort in the class. Trying to make the group more interactive, I asked, "Who can define a polygon?"

"A dead parrot," came the reply.

—JOEL ALMEIDA

A lonely woman buys a parrot for companionship. After a week, the parrot hasn't uttered a word, so the woman goes back to the pet store and buys it a mirror. Nothing. The next week, she brings home a little ladder. Polly is still incommunicado, so the week after that, she gives it a swing, which elicits not a peep.

A week later, she finds the parrot on the floor of its cage, dying. Summoning up its last breath, the bird whispers, "Don't they have any food at that pet store?"

—LUCILLE ARNELL

Knowing how much an acquaintance despises his wife's parakeet, I was surprised one day to hear him coaxing it to speak. Upon listening more closely, however, I nearly choked holding back my laughter. Now, along with its constant, annoying jabbering, the bird also calls out a suicidal, "Here kitty, kitty, kitty."

—LISA FRENCH

"Hello, Amnesty International?"

Late one afternoon on the London Underground, I found myself sitting next to a man who held an empty birdcage on his lap. Curiosity prompted me to ask if the bird had escaped.

"Oh, no," the man replied. "You see, my working hours are irregular, and we have no telephone in our home, so my wife never knows when to expect me for dinner. I take my homing pigeon along to work every morning and release it as soon as my job is finished. "Dinner'll be ready when I get home," he concluded.

—OIVIND HOLTAN

> A frenchman with a parrot perched on his shoulder walked into a bar. The bartender said, "Wow, that's really neat. Where did you get him?"
>
> "In France," the parrot replied. **"They've got millions of 'em over there."**
>
> —A PRAIRIE HOME COMPANION,
> THE FIFTH ANNUAL JOKE SHOW

A businessman flying first class is sitting next to a parrot. The plane takes off, and the parrot orders a Glenlivet, neat. The businessman asks for a Coke. After a few minutes, the bird yells, "Where's my scotch? Give me my scotch!"

The flight attendant rushes over with their drinks. Later, they order another round. Again, the bird gives the crew grief for being slow, and the businessman joins in: "Yeah, the service stinks!"

Just then, the flight attendant grabs the pair, opens the hatch, and throws them out of the plane. As they hurtle toward the ground, the parrot says to the terrified man, "Wow, that took a lot of guts for a guy with no wings."

It was moving day for a New York company, and one junior executive was seen hurrying into the spanking new office skyscraper carrying a caged canary and a large rock. Asked about this, he explained glumly that the windows in his antiseptic new office wouldn't open.

"If the air conditioning ever stops," he went on, "we'll all suffocate. That's why I have this canary. If he keels over, I'll know we're getting low on air—and then *boom*, my rock's going through that window!"

—ARTURO F. GONZALEZ

❤ ❤ ❤ ❤ ❤ ❤ ❤ ❤ ❤ ❤

Jim strolls into the paint section of a hardware store and walks up to the assistant.

"I'd like a pint of canary-colored paint," he says.

"Sure," the clerk replies. "Mind if I ask what it's for?"

"My parakeet," says Jim. "See, I want to enter him in a canary contest. He sings so sweet I know he's sure to win."

"Well, you can't do that, man!" the assistant says. "The chemicals in the paint will almost certainly kill the poor thing!"

"No they won't," Jim replies.

"Listen, buddy, I'll bet you ten bucks your parakeet dies if you try to paint him."

"You're on," says Jim.

Two days later he comes back looking very sheepish and lays $10 on the counter.

"So the paint killed him?"

"Indirectly," says Jim. "He seemed to handle the paint okay, but he didn't survive the sanding between coats."

In good weather, my friend Mark always let his yellow-naped Amazon parrot, Nicky, sit on the balcony of his tenth-floor apartment. One morning, Nicky flew away, much to Mark's dismay. He searched and called for the bird, with no luck.

The next day when Mark returned from work, the phone rang. "Is this Mark?" The caller asked. "You're going to think this is crazy, but there's a bird outside on my balcony saying, 'Hello, this is Mark.' Then it recites this phone number and says, 'I can't come to the phone right now, but if you will leave a message at the tone, I will call you back.'"

Nicky's cage had been kept in the same room as Mark's answering machine.

—ANNE R. NEILSON

"Yes, he talks, but he prefers texts or e-mail."

❤ ❤ ❤ ❤ ❤ ❤ ❤ ❤ ❤ ❤

My parents had a budgie called Joey. He was a talkative bird, although his repertoire was limited to "Hello" and "Who's a pretty boy?"

When my parents went on vacation, a friend and her husband, George, offered to watch Joey. He came home full of life and happy to chat at the end of the week.

However, it was soon obvious that Joey's vocabulary had been extended during his stay. He now squawked in an outraged tone, "Stop it, George!"

—GARTH BUCKLAND

A chinese housewife filed for divorce on the grounds that her husband was having an affair. The woman became suspicious when every time the phone rang, her myna bird spouted things like "Divorce," "I love you" and "Be patient."

—FROM *IDIOTS IN LOVE* BY LELAND GREGORY (ANDREWS MCMEEL)

When my kid sister and my mother bought three exotic birds, they named them This, That and The Other. After a few months, This died, and they buried the bird in the backyard. A few more months later, The Other passed away and they buried it next to This. Then the last bird died. Mom called my sister and tearfully announced, "Well, I guess that's That."

—GLORIA VITULANO

A burglar invaded a home in Los Angeles and tied everyone up. But a pet parakeet quietly opened its cage door, flew to the phone, pushed off the receiver and dialed the police with its beak. The desk sergeant answered and the parakeet chirped desperately: "Pretty baby! Pretty baby!"

—ROBERT J. HERGUTH

Mother to young son:
"Your parrot flew away while you were at school."
"I'm not surprised," sighed the boy. "When I was studying geography yesterday, he sat on my shoulder and closely examined the atlas."

Passing through London, a Frenchman buys a talking parrot. A week later the pet shop receives an outraged letter from the customer: The bird won't utter a word. The conscientious shopkeeper catches a train to Paris and visits the customer. He asks the parrot: "So, Jocko, have you lost your voice?" "No sir, but I don't think anyone should be expected to learn French in a week, replied the bird."

— M. WIDMER

A worried Russian went to the police and reported that his parrot was missing.
"Is it a talking bird?" the police asked.
"Yes, but opinions he expresses are his own, and do not reflect those of the owner."

A woman trained her parrot to give instructions to the tradesmen that called at her house.
One day the coalman came to make a delivery. "Ten sacks please," said the parrot.
"You're a clever bird being able to talk," said the coalman as he finished the delivery.
"Yes," replied the parrot. "And I can count too. Bring the other sack."

—BRIAN JOHNSTON

Mrs. Van Horn inherited Penrod, a parrot that used dirty words. After several embarrassing experiences, she told her minister about the problem.

"I have a female parrot who is a saint," he said. "She sits on her perch and prays all day. Bring your parrot over, mine will be a good influence."

The woman brought Penrod to the minister's home. When the cages were placed together, Penrod cried, "Hi, baby! How about a little loving?"

"Great!" replied the female parrot, "That's just what I've been praying for."

—LARRY WILDE

Actor Ward Bond liked to tell of the man who went into a pet shop to buy a parrot. The shop owner pointed to a colorful specimen and said, "This is a fine talking bird. For years he was the pet of a famous movie producer, weren't you, Polly?"

"Yes, sir!" screamed the parrot. "Yes, yes, yes, yes, indeed! You are absolutely right. Yes, sir!"

—FRANK GORSHI

Trying to eclipse his brother's gift of a Cadillac, a Hollywood producer paid $10,000 for an amazing mynah bird to give his mother on her birthday. The bird spoke 11 languages and sang grand opera. On the night of her birthday he called her long distance.

**"What did you think of the bird, Mama?" he asked.
"Delicious!" she said.**

—EARL WILSON

A little old lady went into a pet shop and saw a lovely-looking parrot. "I would like to buy that handsome bird, please," she said to the owner.

"Oh, you don't want him," the man replied. "He uses some pretty terrible language. Why don't you get a puppy or a cat?"

"I want that parrot!" the woman insisted, and proceeded to put her money on the counter. The owner shrugged his shoulders and made the sale.

When the woman returned home, she started playing with her new friend. She was petting him and poking at his feathers when all of a sudden he started swearing a blue streak. The woman was so shocked that she grabbed the parrot and stuck him in the refrigerator.

When she took the shivering bird out later, she warned him that every time he used bad language he'd be put back where it was cold. The parrot's behavior was pretty good for a couple days, but then one morning while the cat was putting her paw through his cage, he got really mad and started cursing again.

This time, the woman grabbed the bird and stuck him in the freezer. As he sat there shivering and looking around, he saw a frozen turkey right next to him. "Egad!" squawked the parrot, "What did you say?"

—MARIAN B. WISE

As I was walking through a variety store, I stopped at the pet department to look at some parakeets. In one cage a green bird lay on his back, one foot hooked oddly into the cage wire. I was about to alert the saleswoman to the bird's plight when I noticed a sign taped to the cage: "No, I am not sick. No, I am not dead. No, my leg is not stuck in the cage. I just like to sleep this way."

—JOAN DEZEEUW

"QUOTABLE QUOTES

"That's what the cat said to the canary when he swallowed him— 'You'll be all right.'"

—ALVAH BESSIE

"She was not quite what you would call refined. She was not quite what you would call unrefined. She was the kind of person that keeps a parrot."

—MARK TWAIN

"Live in such a way that you would not be ashamed to sell your parrot to the town gossip."

—WILL ROGERS

"I know of only one bird—the parrot—that talks; and it can't fly very high."

—WILBUR WRIGHT

"I hope you love birds too. It is economical. It saves going to heaven."

—EMILY DICKINSON

"God loved the birds and invented trees. Man loved the birds and invented cages."

—JACQUES DEVAL, *AFIN DE VIVRE BEL ET BIEN*

"Did St. Francis really preach to the birds? Whatever for? If he really liked birds he would have done better to preach to the cats."

—REBECCA WEST

"We can all learn something from the parrot, which is content to repeat what it hears without trying to make a good story out of it."

—MALVINA G. VOGEL, EDITOR

♥ ♥ ♥ ♥ ♥ ♥ ♥ ♥ ♥ ♥ ♥

The pet shop customer couldn't believe his good fortune. The parrot he had just bought could recite Shakespeare's sonnets, imitate opera stars and intone Homer's epic poems in Greek. And he cost only $600.

Once the man got the bird home, however, not another word passed his beak. After three weeks the disconsolate customer returned to the shop and asked for his money back.

"When we had this bird," said the proprietor, "he could recite poetry and sing like an angel. Now you want me to take him back when he's no longer himself? Well, all right. Out of the goodness of my heart I'll give you $100."

Reluctantly the man accepted his loss. Just as the door shut behind him he heard the parrot say to the shop owner, "Don't forget—my share is $250."

—A. A. HENDERSON

"I promise. That bird is so well behaved, you can take it anywhere," the pet-store owner assured the woman. Delighted, she took her parrot to church. Things were great until, halfway through the sermon, the bird blurted, "It's damn cold in here!" Embarrassed, the woman ran out and went to the pet store. "This 'good bird' swore in church today," she told the shop owner.

"I'm sorry. It sometimes does that in new environments," he explained. "Next time, grab its feet and swing it over your head a few times. That should stop it." The next week the woman and her parrot were in church when the bird yelled, "It's damn cold in here!" Quickly, the woman grabbed the bird and swung it above her head six times. Then she put the bird back on her shoulder and sat down.

"Damn," the bird said. "It's windy too."

♥ ♥ ♥ ♥ ♥ ♥ ♥ ♥ ♥ ♥ ♥

Late one night a burglar broke into a house.
He froze when he heard a loud voice say,
"Jesus is watching!" Silence returned to the house, so
the burglar crept forward.

"Jesus is watching!" the voice boomed again. The
robber stopped dead in his tracks and frantically looked
all around. He spotted a parrot in a cage.

"Was that you?" asked the burglar. "Yes," answered the
parrot. The criminal sighed in relief and asked, "What's
your name?"

"Clarence," said the bird.

"That's a dumb name for a parrot," sneered the burglar.
"What idiot named you Clarence?"

"The same idiot who named the
Rottweiler Jesus."

A lady would like to have a parrot to keep her company.
She went to the Sunday market in Bangkok to look for one. At
a pet shop she saw a bird cage. The sign on the cage read: "Pull
the right leg, the bird will greet you. Pull the left leg, the bird
will sing." The lady amazingly asked, "What if I pull both legs?"
While the shop owner was trying to come up with an answer,
the bird replied, "You do that and I will fall off the beam!"

—WUTHICHAI NA-PATALUNG

Eric, a yellow-headed parrot that delighted customers in a shoe store in Houston, Texas, with such phrases as "telephone line one," "rock 'n' roll," and "Polly want a cracker," was stolen. The parrot turned into a stool pigeon when he was found in someone else's apartment. The officers, greeted with "hello Laura" and "hello Eric," checked stolen-parrot reports and turned up the name of Laura, owner of the shoe store. She was summoned to see if the bird was hers. When she arrived, the parrot became very excited, flapping its wings and swinging wildly inside its cage. "Eric just started, screaming "Laura," she said. I didn't have to identify him. He identified me."

After he bought a parakeet, my husband spent long, futile hours trying to teach the bird to talk. One morning about three o'clock I heard parakeet noises and woke my husband.

"That crazy bird of yours is in the room!" I exclaimed.

We looked everywhere and finally found the bird sleeping peacefully in his cage downstairs. This mystery repeated itself two more nights, and I was a nervous wreck.

The next night I locked the bedroom door. At two o'clock I awoke again to that unnerving chirping. Very quietly I switched on the lights. There lay my husband, sound asleep and chirping his heart out. The bird had taught my husband his language!

—MRS. JACK PENZENSTADLER

Our curiosity was aroused by our neighbors' parakeet, whose raucous warnings, "No handholding! No kissing!" shattered the quiet of their living room. He'd been trained, our friends explained, to chaperone their teenage daughter's parties.

—MAUD NOBRIGA

As a single parent, I know that my ten-year-old daughter has learned to do without many extras. Sometime ago, to make things up to her, I promised to buy her toys as soon as I got a raise. A while later, my boss went on vacation and arranged for me to watch his dog, cats and parrot.

The night before he was due back, we went to feed the animals for the last time. As my daughter busied herself with the parrot, I couldn't believe my ears. She was bombarding the hapless bird with: "Mommy needs a raise! Mommy needs a raise! Mommy needs a raise!"

I got the raise; she got the toys.

—REGINA WIEGAND

♥ ♥ ♥ ♥ ♥ ♥ ♥ ♥ ♥ ♥

There's a story making the rounds that involves a carpet layer who had worked all day installing wall-to-wall carpeting. When he noticed a lump under the carpet in the middle of the living room, he felt his shirt pocket for his cigarettes—they were gone.

He was not about to take up the carpet, so he went outside for a two-by-four. Tamping down cigarettes with it would be easy. Once the lump was smoothed, the man gathered up his tools and carried them to his truck. Then two things happened simultaneously.

He saw his cigarettes on the seat of the truck, and over his shoulder he heard the voice of the woman to whom the carpet belonged.

"Have you seen anything of my parakeet?" she asked plaintively.

—FRANK RHOADES

A parrot was up for sale at an auction. The bidding proceeded briskly, and soon a winner was announced. When paying, the high bidder asked the auctioneer if the parrot could speak.

"Sure can," replied the auctioneer, "it was the parrot that was bidding against you."

—ANNE H. WINSNES

A pet-shop owner figured out a way to sell his talking parrots. He has a sign over each, reading:

"Suggested for mature audiences only."

—EARL WILSON

♥ ♥ ♥ ♥ ♥ ♥ ♥ ♥ ♥ ♥ ♥

A pet shop owner is asked for a bird that can talk and sing. He shows the customer a scrawny-looking bird with a price tag of $3,000.

"How can it be worth that much?" says the customer.

"That bird can sing the complete works of Elgar," replies the owner. "Or you could try this one." He reveals a second bird, even thinner than the first, with faded plumage. It is priced at $5,000.

"Come on," says the customer. "What's so special about this one?"

"It can reproduce all of Verdi's operas note-perfect," says the owner. "But I have one other that might interest you." The third bird is in a sorry state, bald, rheumy-eyed and weak with age. The customer looks at the price tag.

"$16,000?" he says. "What does this one do?"

The owner shakes his head. "To tell you the truth, we don't know yet. But the other two call him 'Maestro.'"

—MARION CARLSON

My husband and I, newlyweds and animal lovers, bought an Amazon parrot when we moved to our first apartment. Since pets were not allowed, we had to keep Juju a secret. Soon our little friend became an accomplished talker and mimic. His favorite trick was returning parrot kisses after I commanded in a loud voice: "Give me a kiss! Give me a big smooch!"

Within days Juju was repeating those words incessantly, doing his parrot-perfect imitation of me: "Give me a kiss! Give me a big smooch!"

I hadn't realized how thin the walls were until the day I found this note on my door: "Look, lady—I realize you're newlyweds, but give the poor guy a break!"

—BARBARA JANNATPOUR

♥ ♥ ♥ ♥ ♥ ♥ ♥ ♥ ♥ ♥

The ad on a bulletin board read: For sale: African gray parrot $500. This species is one of the best talkers." Someone had jotted on it in pencil: **"Ask him if he's worth $500."**

—EDWARD J. RAYMOND

A man bought a parrot for $1,000. Sure, it cost plenty, but this bird had talent. Polly not only had a big vocabulary, but could also rattle on in five languages. The pet shop promised to deliver the bird that afternoon.

After work, the proud owner rushed home and asked if it had arrived. It had, his wife told him.

"Where is it?" he asked excitedly.

"In the oven," she replied.

"My god!" said the husband. "In the oven? Why? That bird knows five languages!"

"Well," asked his wife, "why didn't he speak up?"

—JOHN COSTELLO

The kids had been driving me nuts, asking me to buy them a talking bird, until I finally got them a parrot. We named him Wilbur and tried to teach him some words, but all he would say was, "Hello. Hello."

Over and over again my older son tried to get Wilbur to say, "Jeff is the greatest." Nothing. My husband tried with "Give this guy a raise." Nothing. I took a turn with "Clean your room." Still nothing.

Yesterday Wilbur finally started talking. During dinner all we heard was "He did it. No, he did it," and then "Get out of my room!"

—FELICE R. PRAGER

♥ ♥ ♥ ♥ ♥ ♥ ♥ ♥ ♥ ♥

The canary I bought for my daughter some months before suddenly stopped singing and sat huddled on its perch. Not knowing what was the matter with it, I called the Arnold sisters, who raise canaries and from whom I had bought ours. Miss Agatha, aged 78, answered the telephone. When I described the bird's symptoms, she immediately recommended that we get it a mate. "It's spring," she said, "and the bird is lonely."

I protested that I didn't want two birds, and then launched into a tale about a friend who lost one of a pair of lovebirds and solved the problem by putting a mirror in the cage as company for the other. "Maybe," I added brightly, "that would satisfy the canary."

There was a pause, and then Miss Agatha said softly, "Would that satisfy you, Mrs. Smith?"

—MRS. ROSS W. SMITH

Randy the dishwasher repairman was given specific instructions concerning the woman's two pets.

"The Rottweiler won't hurt you, even though it looks fierce, but whatever you do, don't talk to the parrot." Randy let himself in and set to work, and the dog just lay quietly on the carpet. But the parrot mocked him mercilessly the whole time.

"Wow, you're pretty fat," the bird would say. "Hey, fatso, you couldn't change the batteries in a flashlight, let alone fix a dishwasher."

Before long, Randy had had enough. "You know, bird, you think you're pretty smart for someone with a brain the size of a pea."

The parrot was silent for a moment, and then, with a gleam in its eye, said, "All right. Get him, Spike."

—TERRI BOAS

❤ ❤ ❤ ❤ ❤ ❤ ❤ ❤ ❤ ❤ ❤

In the pet shop of a large department store in
Portland, OR., I stopped in front of the
cage of a mynah bird. The bird cocked its
head and said, "Hello."

I was surprised and didn't say anything.
After a short pause the bird said,
"What's the matter, can't you talk?"

—ELGAR P. BEADERSTADT

When Rich, who graduated last June from West Point,
reluctantly agreed to postpone his marriage until he returned
from foreign duty, he proceeded to devote considerable time and
effort to reducing the calculated risk of the agreement. I saw the
result when I attended his girl Ann's graduation exercises at a
Massachusetts college.

His present to Ann was a parakeet whose cage bore the
inscription: "My ambassador for the duration. Love, Rich."

Ambassador took but a moment to smooth his feathers,
then, in a remarkable imitation of Rich's voice, began chanting,
"Remember Rich! Remember Rich! Remember Rich!"

—TAY COOK

"How come you're so well informed about your neighbor's
doings?

"He went on vacation and I looked after his parrot for two
weeks."

—ALBERT W. BROMBACHER

♥ ♥ ♥ ♥ ♥ ♥ ♥ ♥ ♥ ♥ ♥

"**F**reddie," read the advertisement I had composed for our local newspaper, "a recently widowed lovebird, desperately seeks a new mate, preferably a gentle young lady who has been hand raised."

I gave the text to the receptionist at the newspaper office and waited while she read it. Surprisingly she glanced up at me disdainfully. "Of course you want this placed in the Personals?"

"Heavens, no!" I hastened to assure her. "The Pet section." Freddie's mate, a lovebird, had escaped from their cage a few months earlier, and he was lonely.

—RAYMOND R. FIELDING

 What do you get when you cross a tiger with a canary? ?

I don't know. But when it sings, you'd better listen.

—NAVNEET KUMAR

Then there was the old gal who died and left $20,000 to her dog and cat.

"But they're going to have trouble trying to collect," said one chap, "I understand her parakeet is contesting the will."

—CHRIS HOBSON

The devoted couple doted on their peg gray thrushes. One day the female flew out while the cage was being cleaned. The wife was disconsolate, and her husband offered to buy another female thrush on his way home.

"What?" she cried, more disconsolate than ever. "How can you think of remarrying the moment she is gone?"

—CHIK KA KEUNG

As the manager of a bird store, part of my job is to trim the wings and nails of our customers' feathered friends. One day a woman brought in her pet parrot. While working, I lost my grip on the bird and he bit down hard on my finger. I almost let out a yell, but stopped myself before saying something I might regret. Right then our store pet, a very vocal parrot, let out a stream of obscenities. Horrified, I started to make apologies, but the customer held up her hand and said, "I think he just took the words right out of your mouth!"

—LYNN K. CHURCH

❤ ❤ ❤ ❤ ❤ ❤ ❤ ❤ ❤ ❤ ❤

Near the main entrance to Billy Rose's Aquacade at the New York World's Fair was a small exhibit with a sign over the door which read: "Billy Rose's Pet Shop."

Every time Billy went to his great spectacle, he passed this place. He finally decided to get his lawyer to put a stop to the use of his name to peddle bullfrogs and tropical fish. The two marched belligerently into the offending establishment.

"I'm Billy Rose," he announced, "and this is my lawyer."

"Oh, yes, I was expecting you, Mr. Rosenberg," replied the pet-shop proprietor (Rosenberg is Billy's real name).

"Well," Billy went on, "I want you to stop trading on my name to sell your goldfish. Otherwise, we will take action."

The man reached under the counter and brought out his birth certificate, explaining, "I thought you might want to see it."

His square name was Billy Rose. The two callers studied it a minute and then Billy asked, "How much are your canaries?"

"Five dollars each," the man said.

"Let me have two with a cage." Billy walked out with his new pets.

—JOHN WHEELER

There's a magician who works his show on a cruise ship. After a while, the captain's parrot understands how the magician does every trick and starts shouting, "Look, it's not the same hat," "He's hiding the flowers under the table," or "Hey, why are all the cards the ace of spades?" The magician is furious, but can't do anything against the captain's parrot. Then the ship sinks, and the magician and the parrot find themselves on a piece of wood, staring at each other with hatred. This goes on for days. Finally, the parrot can't hold back: "Okay, I give up. Where's the ship?"

—BASIL HENDRICKSON

♥ ♥ ♥ ♥ ♥ ♥ ♥ ♥ ♥ ♥ ♥

As a professional magician, I travel quite a bit. A few years ago, I was flying back home through Pearson airport in Toronto. I checked my baggage and a pet carrier containing several white doves, then mentioned to the young lady behind the counter that I was a magician and that these birds were part of my act.

She looked at me and asked, "Have they flown before?"

"Well," I replied, "they are birds!"

—DALE DOWNING

An elderly man sitting on a park bench was joined by a youth sporting multi-colored spiked hair so bizarre that the man couldn't stop staring at it. "What's the matter, old man?" the youth asked sarcastically. "Never done aything wild in your life?"

"Well, in a moment of alcohol-induced madness, I once made love to a parrot," the man replied. "I'm just wondering if you're my son."

—LISA MCDERMOTT

Tell me, can that parrot talk?

He's just asked the same about you.

—WWW.KULICHKI.RU

A desperate voice calls the police by phone: "Help, come quickly! A cat has just entered my house!"

"A cat? Don't be afraid. There's not need to worry about a cat."

"Please! It's a tragedy!"

"To whom am I speaking?"

"It's the parrot!"

—GILMAR DE OLIVEIRA DORNELAS, JR.

♥ ♥ ♥ ♥ ♥ ♥ ♥ ♥ ♥ ♥ ♥

A man dreamed of owning a parrot. He had never seen one, but had heard that it was a bird that talked. A friend suggested that he visit an aviary of a person he knew, adding that he would telephone to say that he was sending him there. The man went to the aviary, but the owner, who had no parrots at the time, and knew that the man had never seen one, gave him an owl.

Sometime later, the man saw his friend. "How is the parrot?" his friend inquired.

"It's beautiful and I love it!" the man replied.

"So, is it talking yet?"

"To be honest, it doesn't talk. But when I speak to it, it pays close attention to what I say."

—ANTÓNIO DOMINGOS PINHEIRO

That's a
pet?

Animals are such
agreeable friends—
they ask no questions,
they pass no criticisms.

—GEORGE ELIOT, *MR. GILFIL'S LOVE STORY*

"While I was watching the dog so he wouldn't eat my homework, the hamster went and shredded it for his nest!"

My little nephew came home from school all excited because a beautiful white rabbit named Snowball, used in his nature-study class, was to be given to the lucky child whose name was pulled out of a hat the next day. To participate in the drawing, each child had to bring a note from home saying his parents would let him keep the animal if he won it. The thought of another pet to cope with unnerved me but, rationalizing that our chances of losing were pretty good with 28 other pupils in the class, I gave him the note. That afternoon, the boy rushed in and announced ecstatically that Snowball was his.

"You mean that, out of the whole class, you won the bunny?" I asked incredulously.

"Well, not exactly," he replied. "I was the only one with a note."

—GERTRUDE H. ANDERSON

The kids had been begging for weeks, so their mom finally gave in and bought them a hamster. But just as she had feared, she was the one who wound up taking care of it. One evening, exasperated, she sat them down and asked, "Why did you even want that darn thing? How many times do you think it would have died if I hadn't been looking after it for you?"

"I don't know," her son said. "Once?"

—ADAM JOSHUA SMARGON

An adorable little girl walked into my pet shop and asked, "Excuse me, do you have any rabbits here?"

"I do," I answered, and leaning down to her eye level I asked, "Did you want a white rabbit or would you rather have a soft, fuzzy black rabbit?"

She shrugged. "I don't think my python really cares."

—CINDY PATTERSON

♥ ♥ ♥ ♥ ♥ ♥ ♥ ♥ ♥ ♥ ♥

Two campers are hiking in the woods when one is bitten on the rear end by a rattlesnake. "I'll go into town for a doctor," the other says. He runs ten miles to a small town and finds the only doctor delivering a baby.

"I can't leave," the doctor says. "But here's what to do. Take a knife, cut a little X where the bite is, suck out the poison and spit it on the ground."

The guy runs back to his friend, who is in agony. "What did the doctor say?" the victim cries.

"He says you're gonna die."

My friend's husband, Ray, is a state trooper and enjoys sharing the excuses people use when stopped for speeding. One day, however, the tables were turned. Ray maintains an aquarium of exotic fish, and a prized specimen had threatened to turn belly up. The off-duty officer called a pet store, and they advised him to immediately purchase a special additive that would correct the water's pH.

Ray and his wife jumped into the car and rushed to the store. A state trooper signaled them to pull over.

"Go ahead," Ray's wife said. "Tell him you've got a sick fish!"

—DEBRA MCVEY

A Hollywood producer who keeps a goldfish in a bowl on his desk was recently asked why.

"Because," he replied glumly, **"I like to see something around here with its mouth open not asking for a raise."**

—BOB HULL

♥ ♥ ♥ ♥ ♥ ♥ ♥ ♥ ♥ ♥ ♥

 What's a snake's favorite opera?
Wriggeletto

— AROON PURIE

I was helping my daughter scrub her pet pig—250 pounds of squealing indignation—in preparation for an upcoming state fair. The phone in the barn rang and I grabbed it.

"Hello," I screamed above the earsplitting din. No answer. "Hello!" I tried again.

"I can hear you," came the amused reply of Jean, the mother of three active preschool boys, "I just thought I'd never hear anybody whose kids made more noise than mine when their mother got on the phone."

—MARY HAVENS

Poster on a power pole in San Francisco: "Lost: Pet aardvark. Description: Basically your everyday, common aardvark. Long, pinkish snout, one tail, hairy in spots, not overly attractive. Waddles·with noticeable limp in right rear leg. Answers to the name Sergio. Last seen on a leisurely stroll down Sacramento Street. Is trailing a three-foot-long leash attached to a rhinestone collar. Your reward: getting rid of it."

—HERB CAEN

A guy walks into a bar with a lizard on his shoulder. "What do you call that?" asks the bartender.

"Tiny," says the guy. "Because he's my newt."

♥ ♥ ♥ ♥ ♥ ♥ ♥ ♥ ♥ ♥ ♥

Did you know goldfish don't like to watch television?
Yeah, they're afraid they might get hooked.

—JOHN SIERZANT

A friend of mine received a pet ferret as a gift from his girlfriend. This small, weasel-like creature is very tame, but it's small wonder that heads turn when the adorable animal is walked on its leash along the city streets. Its name? Ferret Fawcett, of course!

—TIMOTHY STEWART

A vicious bite from one of his prize-winning show rabbits sent my 15-year-old son to the emergency room. The doctor and attendants who cleaned the wound and bandaged his hand were clearly amused about how he got the injury.

As we were leaving the ER, they handed us a sheaf of papers that included a prescription for antibiotics, a wound-care information sheet and a recipe for rabbit stew.

—JIM LORD

While I was having coffee with a friend, her teenage daughter rushed into the house all excited.

"Mother, could I get a pet rabbit?" she asked.

"Well, you could," said my friend, "but it would cost you about 500 dollars a month to keep it."

The girl looked at her mother in disbelief. "Mom," she said, "the whole rabbit only costs four dollars."

"Yes," said my friend, "but you're not keeping it in my house, so you'd have to rent an apartment."

—M.R. SMITH

"Is it just me...or do you feel like you're in a snow globe?"

❤ ❤ ❤ ❤ ❤ ❤ ❤ ❤ ❤ ❤ ❤

Steve, a lonely bachelor, decided to get himself a pet. At the pet store, he told the shopkeeper he wanted something unusual. The shopkeeper suggested an exotic centipede he'd just received. Steve readily agreed, bought the centipede and a small box for it to live in, then went home happy.

That evening he decided to go out, so he asked the centipede, "Want to come down to Frank's place for a drink?" There was no answer from the box.

A few minutes later he asked again, still no reply. Finally, he hollered at the box: "Hey! You in there! Do you want to go down to Frank's for a drink with me?"

"I heard you the first time!" said a small, irritated voice.

"I'm putting on my shoes!"

♥ ♥ ♥ ♥ ♥ ♥ ♥ ♥ ♥ ♥ ♥

My teenage daughter and I were in the yard playing with our new pet nanny goat that was exploring and nibbling everything in sight. We soon noticed that she ignored our lush green lawn and preferred to pick out harmful-looking weeds and other non-nourishing tidbits. "What a strange animal," I commented. "She ignores all the stuff that's good for her and instead eats all the junk food that's lying around."

"Oh, she's not so weird," my daughter replied. "She's no different from any other normal kid!"

—ANNA HOUSTON

The devout cowboy lost his favorite Bible while he was mending fences out on the range.

Three weeks later a cow walked up to him carrying the Bible in its mouth. The cowboy couldn't believe his eyes. He took the book out of the cow's mouth, raised his eyes heavenward and exclaimed, "It's a miracle!"

"Not really," said the cow. "Your name is written inside the cover."

— ROMAN WILBERT

My son's teacher has a miniature pet donkey that accompanied the family on an 800-mile trek along the Appalachian Trail. His name? **Donkey Oatie.**

—CATHIE GLEBA

❤ ❤ ❤ ❤ ❤ ❤ ❤ ❤ ❤ ❤ ❤

A man was admiring the tropical fish in the pet shop where I used to work. When I offered my assistance, he mentioned that his new wife was a fish fancier. After I showed him around, he shouted, "There she is! That's the one I'll take."

As I scooped out a large, sluggish goldfish with a gray splotch at the top of its head, the man exclaimed, "My bride will love this! She's always wanted to know what my first wife looked like!"

—JOAN INGLIS

Just as our neighbor was experiencing a minor household emergency, the telephone rang. She picked up the receiver and hurriedly exclaimed, "I can't talk now, our white mouse is loose in the kitchen and I have to catch him before the cat does!"

She let the receiver dangle from the hook for a good five minutes. When she did get back to the phone, it was only to hear an unfamiliar voice on the other end say, "Excuse me, lady, I knew I had a wrong number, but I just had to find out—who got the mouse?"

—R. FRASER PORTER

A turtle is crossing the road when he's mugged by two snails. When the police show up, they ask him what happened. The shaken turtle replies, "I don't know. It all happened so fast."

—DEBBY CARTER

 What's stranger than seeing a catfish?
Seeing a goldfish bowl.

QUOTABLE QUOTES

"I think there's something great and generic about goldfish. They're everybody's first pet."

—PAUL RUDD

"I don't believe in reincarnation, and I didn't believe in it when I was a hamster."

—SHANE RITCHIE

"My roommate got a pet elephant. Then it got lost. It's in the apartment somewhere."

—STEPHEN WRIGHT

"Dogs look up to you; cats look down on you; pigs treat you as an equal."

—WINSTON CHURCHILL

"Try to be like the turtle—at ease in your own shell."

—BILL COPELAND

"No animal should ever jump up on the dining room furniture unless absolutely certain that he can hold his own in the conversation."

—FRAN LEBOWITZ

"When I was a kid, if a guy got killed in a Western movie I always wondered who got his horse."

—GEORGE CARLIN

"My favorite animal is the turtle. For the turtle to move, it has to stick its neck out."

—RUTH WESTHEIMER

"It's hard to lose weight when I need to stay bigger than anything my pet python can swallow."

♥ ♥ ♥ ♥ ♥ ♥ ♥ ♥ ♥ ♥ ♥

An old lady was taking a pet tortoise by train from London to Edinburgh and wanted to know whether she ought to buy a dog ticket for it, as one has to do in England when taking a cat by train, because cats officially count as dogs.

"No, mum," said the ticket inspector, "cats is dogs, and dogs is dogs, and squirrels in cages is parrots, but this here turtle is a insect, and we won't charge you nothing."

—ROBERT GRAVES

My young son and I spent much time in pet shops looking for just the right fish for his aquarium and for snails to keep the tank clean. One day he came home from a shopping trip all excited to tell me he had discovered some African frogs that really did a good job cleaning the aquarium.

"Good," I said, "then you won't have to buy any snails."

"Oh, yes," he said, "I have to buy them too. Those frogs don't do windows."

—MRS. ROGER RAYMOND

A computer nerd is crossing the road when he sees a frog who opens its mouth and starts talking.

"If you kiss me," the frog says, "I'll turn into a beautiful princess, stay with you for a week and do anything you want."

The guy smiles and puts the frog in his pocket.

"Did you hear me?" asks the frog. "A beautiful princess? For a week?"

"Look," says the nerd, "I haven't got time for a girlfriend. But a talking frog—now that's cool."

—STUART WIGNALL

As I strolled through an import shop, I wondered how the proprietors kept customers from sifting through the neatly stacked displays of woven baskets. Then I spotted this sign:

"Please do not rummage through the baskets. We haven't seen our pet cobra in weeks."

—B.V.C.

My brother adopted a snake named Slinky, whose most disagreeable trait was eating live mice. Once I was pressed into going to the pet store to buy Slinky's dinner.

The worst part of this wasn't choosing the juiciest-looking creatures or turning down the clerk who wanted to sell me vitamins to ensure their longevity. The hardest part was carrying the poor things out in a box bearing the words "Thank you for giving me a home."

—JOANNE MITCHELL

A guy finds a sheep wandering in his neighborhood and takes it to the police station. The desk sergeant says, "Why don't you just take it to the zoo?"

The next day, the sergeant spots the same guy walking down the street—with the sheep.

"I thought I told you to take that sheep to the zoo," the sergeant says.

"I know what you told me," the guy responds. "Yesterday I took him to the zoo. Today I'm taking him to the movies."

—TAMARA CUMMINGS

♥ ♥ ♥ ♥ ♥ ♥ ♥ ♥ ♥ ♥ ♥

My aunt recently had to explain to her four-year-old daughter, Faith, that their pet rabbit had died. Faith thought about this news for a minute, then said, "Well, I guess now I can sing that song from my CD."

"What song is that, honey?" asked my aunt.

With a mournful expression on her face, Faith began to sing, "Bring back, bring back, oh bring back my bunny to me, to me..."

—KATHLEEN SPARKES

On a recent trip to the post office,
I took a few minutes to read the notices posted on the public bulletin board in the lobby. One in particular caught my eye.
It read: "Lost in post-office parking lot, small boa constrictor, family pet, will not attack. Reward."

Below the notice someone had written, in what appeared to be very shaky handwriting:

"Please, would you mind posting another notice when you find your boa? Thank you."

—SUSAN ESBENSEN

❤ ❤ ❤ ❤ ❤ ❤ ❤ ❤ ❤ ❤ ❤

Why did the frog wear a mask to the bank?
He said he wanted to "rob-bit."

Scientists at the University of Pennsylvania School of Medicine announced they have found a cure for baldness in mice. This is great news. Nothing looks more ridiculous than a mouse with a comb-over.

—BEN WALSH

The injury to our piglet wasn't serious, but it did require stitches. So I sent my teenage daughter back into the farmhouse to get needle and thread and bring it to me, while I looked after the squealing animal.

Ten minutes later she still hadn't returned.

"What are you doing?" I called out.

She yelled back, "Looking for the pink thread."

—JUNE HALEY

"What is that sound?" a woman visiting our nature center asked.

"It's the frogs trilling for a mate," Patti, the naturalist, explained. "We have a pair in the science room. But since they've been together for so long, they no longer sing to each other."

The woman nodded sympathetically. "The trill is gone."

—KATHYJO TOWNSON

"Well, the kiss didn't work. How about a cuddle?"

♥ ♥ ♥ ♥ ♥ ♥ ♥ ♥ ♥ ♥ ♥

FOR SALE:
"Ferret, likes kids, nice pet, but chewed the guinea
pig's ear off. Also, partially deaf guinea pig."

—BILL PORTER, FROM THE DANVERS, ILL., *SHOPPER*

When a lonely frog consults a fortune-teller, he's told not
to worry.

"You are going to meet a beautiful young girl," she says, "and
she will want to know everything about you."

"That's great!" says the excited frog. "When will I meet her?"

"Next semester," says the psychic, "in biology class."

—ZHANG WENYI

"Hey, peanut butter!" the mouse exclaimed, and then
climbed on top of the lid and started dancing. A second mouse
saw him and asked, "What are you doing?" The first mouse, still
shaking his tail, pointed to the lid. "It says, 'Twist to open.'"

—THOM DELUCA

A guy drives into a ditch, but luckily, a farmer is there to
help. He hitches his horse, Buddy, up to the car and yells, "Pull,
Nellie, pull!" Buddy doesn't move.

"Pull, Buster, pull!" Buddy doesn't budge.

"Pull, Coco, pull!" Nothing.

Then the farmer says, "Pull, Buddy, pull!" And the horse
drags the car out of the ditch.

Curious, the motorist asks the farmer why he kept calling
his horse by the wrong name.

"Buddy's blind," said the farmer. "And if he thought he was
the only one pulling, he wouldn't even try."

—CHARLES LEERHSEN

♥ ♥ ♥ ♥ ♥ ♥ ♥ ♥ ♥ ♥ ♥

A duck walks into a drugstore and asks for a tube of ChapStick. The cashier says to the duck, "That'll be $1.49."

The duck replies, "Put it on my bill!"

The pregnant guppy in the science-room fish tank fascinated my seventh-grade class. We all anxiously awaited the arrival of her babies. But a lesson on human growth and development raised a question for one student.

"Mrs. Townsend," she called out, "how will we know when the fish's water breaks?"

—DANA TOWNSEND

A lonely farm boy returning to an air force recruit training center after his first 48-hour pass carried his pet pig under his arm.

"You can't have a pet in barracks." said the guard at the gate.

"I can keep him under my bunk."

"That's impossible," said the guard. "What about the smell?"

"He'll just have to get used to it like I did."

—DAVE MCINTOSH

There, in the reptiles section of our zoo, a male turtle was on top of a female behaving very, um, affectionately. My daughter was transfixed. She asked, "Mommy?"

Uh-oh, I thought. Here comes The Question. "Yes?" I said.

"Why doesn't he go around?"

—DAWN HOISINGTON

"OK, when I was a kitten I may have lied about where I came from."

❤ ❤ ❤ ❤ ❤ ❤ ❤ ❤ ❤ ❤ ❤

Following the recent mad cow disease scare in our state, one local rancher sought to allay fears by posting this sign: "All our cows have completed anger management classes."

—A. C. BOYETTE

"Can I purchase frogs for my new pond here?" a customer asked at our garden center.

"You don't buy frogs," I explained. "They just sort of choose where they live, then turn up."

"Right..." agreed the gentleman. "And is the same true with fish?"

—SAMANTHA DAVIS

Having lost one of our goldfish, I went to the pet shop to pick a replacement. Among the dozens in the tank, I pointed one out to the shop owner, who stood with net poised.

On seeing the net, the fish darted to the other side of the tank. Pursued by the shop owner, it then darted in the opposite direction. This went on for a while. Due to the frenzy in the tank and the shop owner's stress, I opted instead for any fish, and one was quickly caught.

On revisiting the shop weeks later, I saw a new sign: "Personally chosen fish, 50¢ extra."

—KATHRYN MURRAY

My greatest contribution to humor came when I taught my pet lizard to walk on its hind legs. It was the world's first stand-up chameleon.

—JOHN S. CROSBIE

♥ ♥ ♥ ♥ ♥ ♥ ♥ ♥ ♥ ♥ ♥

I have the most frustrated pet in the world—
a turtle that chases cars.

—ROBERT ORBEN

One day while we were doing yard work, my nine-year-old daughter found a baby snake, and I encouraged her to catch it and put it in a jar. Later she found a huge bullfrog and got another jar to put it in. After dark I told her she would have to set them free. With the frog in one hand and the snake in the other, she started down the porch steps. Suddenly she screamed wildly, dropped both the snake and the frog, and ran into the house.

"What happened?" I asked, my heart thumping.

"Did you see that?" she replied. "That moth almost got me."

—CASSANDRA DALZELL

Squirrels had overrun three churches in town. After much prayer, the elders of the first church determined that the animals were predestined to be there. Who were they to interfere with God's will, they reasoned. Soon, the squirrels multiplied.

The elders of the second church, deciding that they could not harm any of God's creatures, humanely trapped the squirrels and set them free outside of town. Three days later, the squirrels were back.

It was only the third church that succeeded in keeping the pests away. The elders baptized the squirrels and registered them as members of the church. Now they only see them on Christmas and Easter.

❤ ❤ ❤ ❤ ❤ ❤ ❤ ❤ ❤ ❤ ❤

A mother mouse and her baby were scampering across a polished floor when they heard a noise. They hoped it would be a human being, but it turned out to be the family cat. Upon seeing the mice, the cat gave chase. Mama mouse felt a swipe of paw and claw. She turned in her tracks and called out in her loudest voice, "Bow-wow!" and the cat ran off.

Gathering her baby to her and catching her breath, Mama mouse explained, "Now, my child, you see how important a second language is."

—SANDRA J. HULDEN

♥ ♥ ♥ ♥ ♥ ♥ ♥ ♥ ♥ ♥

It's really humid in the woods, so the two hiking buddies remove their shirts and shoes. But when they spot the sign Beware of Bears, one of them stops to put his shoes back on.

"But what's the point?" the other hiker asks. "You can't outrun a bear."

"Actually," says his friend, "all I have to do is outrun you."

—DON PAQUETTE

My niece bought her five-year-old daughter, Kayleigh, a hamster. One day he escaped from his cage. The family turned the house upside down and finally found him. Several weeks later, while Kayleigh was at school, he escaped from his cage again. My niece searched frantically but never found the critter. Hoping to make the loss less painful for Kayleigh, my niece took the cage out of her room. When Kayleigh came home from school that afternoon, she climbed into her mother's lap.

"We've got a serious problem," she announced. "Not only is my hamster gone again, but this time he took the cage."

—PATSY STRINGER

One February, a 13-year-old boy in Mount Airy, N.C., found a turtle near his home, carved his name and address on the shell and turned the turtle loose.

In September, he received a postcard from Ohio that said: "Dear Jeff, I found a small turtle with your name and address on it heading north on U.S. 35 at Jackson, Ohio. **I turned him around; be on the lookout.**"

—JEAN KELLY

❤ ❤ ❤ ❤ ❤ ❤ ❤ ❤ ❤ ❤ ❤

Sharing the two bathrooms in his house with a wife and five daughters has at times been very trying for a close friend of mine. However, his sense of humor has carried him through.

Recently, his two youngest daughters received a large turtle as a gift. They put the new pet in the bathtub while they went looking for more permanent accommodations for it. I was visiting with the man of the house in the living room when the oldest daughter suddenly burst in.

"Daddy!" she screamed, "There's a turtle in the bathtub and he's trying to get out!"

Without even shifting position in his favorite chair, my friend calmed her with,

"Just close your eyes, honey, and hand him a towel."

—BILL GRANT

♥ ♥ ♥ ♥ ♥ ♥ ♥ ♥ ♥ ♥ ♥

A sign over goldfish display: "Wet Pets"

—DILYS JONES

Four jack rabbits are strolling in the prairie. Out of nowhere, a gang of coyotes begins to chase them. So the rabbits run under a huge cactus for refuge.

Then the hungry coyotes surround the cactus. One jack rabbit says to another, "Okay, should we make a run for it, or wait till we outnumber them?

—BENITO F. JUAREZ

"Nice dog. What's its name?" I asked my friend's 10-year-old son.

"Bob," he said.

"And your cat?"

"Bob."

"How do you keep them straight?"

"Well, one is Bob Cat and the other is Bob Barker," the boy answered.

"Tell him your rabbit's name," his father suggested.

The kid smiled and said, "Dennis Hopper."

—MIKE HARRELSON

A farmer wonders how many sheep he has in his field, so he asks his sheepdog to count.

"So what's the verdict?" the farmer asks when the dog is done.

"Forty."

"Huh?" the farmer says, puzzled. "I only had thirty-eight."

"I know," the dog says. "But I rounded them up."

"It's for you."

♥ ♥ ♥ ♥ ♥ ♥ ♥ ♥ ♥ ♥ ♥

During the first week of school, one of my high school science pupils brought me a hamster. To prevent the confusion that always occurs with the appearance of an animal in the classroom, I placed the hamster safely out of sight in the breast pocket of my blouse, where he promptly fell asleep.

All went well until my third-period class, when the hamster awoke and created a small commotion in the pocket. It was then that one of my more perceptive boys turned to a nearby classmate and commented, "It looks like she's got on one of those living bras."

—ANN W. ABERNATHY

A panda walks into a bar, sits down and orders a sandwich. He eats, pulls out a gun and shoots the waiter dead. As the panda stands up to go, the bartender shouts, "Hey! Where are you going? You just shot my waiter and you didn't pay for the food."

The panda yells back, "Hey, man, I'm a panda. Look it up!"

The bartender opens his dictionary to panda: "A tree-climbing mammal of Asian origin, characterized by distinct black and white coloring. Eats shoots and leaves."

Recently, my colleague took a goldfish into her kindergarten classroom for her students. She asked them to suggest names for their new pet. One little fellow seemed deep in thought, so she asked him for his contribution. He looked intently at the small fish, then announced confidently, **"Bait!"**

♥ ♥ ♥ ♥ ♥ ♥ ♥ ♥ ♥ ♥ ♥ ♥

 What do you get when you cross a turtle with a porcupine?

A slow poke.

So I went into a pet shop and said, "Can I buy a goldfish?"

"Do you want an aquarium?" said the shopowner.

"I don't care what star sign it is," I said. "Just give me the fish."

—DORIS POOLE

After years of raising donkeys, an old farmer discovered an unusually intelligent one.

He remembered stories of horses learning to add and subtract by stomping their hooves. Thinking his donkey was smarter than any horse, he went a step further and taught him to multiply and divide.

The farmer was sure the public would pay to see his amazing donkey, so he sold his farm and went on the road, renting booths at fairs to show off the animal's mental prowess.

Unfortunately, he could never find customers who wanted to see his donkey perform. It seems he learned the hard way that nobody likes a smart ass.

—JEFF LISZKA

A guy walks into a bar and there's a horse serving drinks. The horse asks, "What are you staring at? Haven't you ever seen a horse tending bar before?"

The guy says, "It's not that. I just never thought the parrot would sell the place."

♥ ♥ ♥ ♥ ♥ ♥ ♥ ♥ ♥ ♥ ♥ ♥

It's a very tony bar in a hotel in Manhattan. A scruffy guy walks in. The bartender's kind of giving him the eye. The guy comes up to the bar and says, "Yeah, I know I look kind of scruffy, but can I at least get a beer if I show you something really cool?" There's no one else in the place, so the bartender says, "Sure. Why not?"

The guy takes out a little ebony box. He opens it up and takes out a little ebony piano, a little ebony piano bench and a little mouse dressed in black pants. Then he takes out a little ivory box. Out comes a beautiful monarch butterfly. And after the mouse warms up on the piano, the monarch starts singing the famous aria "Un Bel Di" from the opera Madama Butterfly. The music fills the room, and it's so moving that there are tears running down the bartender's cheeks. He gives the man a whole bottle of the best stuff on the top shelf and says, "You know, I'm just moved beyond belief. Why don't you go into show business? Go on Letterman, go on Leno. They'll love this. You'll make a fortune."

The guy says, "No, no, I tried that. They won't touch it."

"What do you mean? It moved me to tears, and I don't even like opera."

"It's really not as good as it seems. The butterfly can't sing a note—the mouse is a ventriloquist."

—ROBERT STANLEY

"I think my goldfish has seizures," a man tells the veterinarian.

"He seems fine now," says the vet.

"Now, sure. But wait till I take him out of the bowl."

—NANCY SEND

♥ ♥ ♥ ♥ ♥ ♥ ♥ ♥ ♥ ♥ ♥

I took my two children to the county fair, and each of them won a chameleon. But after a few weeks, one of the reptiles died. Thinking it would be a good opportunity to teach them about responsibility, I said to the kids, "You know, it probably died of neglect."

"Don't blame me, Dad," my daughter said quickly. "I never touched them."

—CURTIS HOKE

When our pet tortoise, Torty, discovered our newly built rockery, he took a fancy to a round, flat stone about his own size. Throughout the long, hot days of summer he made amorous advances toward it. When we took it away he became extremely distressed and would race round the garden looking for it until it was returned.

Last week I went into the garden and discovered a very interested tortoise inspecting four large, oval pebbles next to the big stone.

"Well," said my husband when I asked him about them. "the poor chap has worked so hard, I thought he deserved some reward for his efforts."

—BARBARA MCGEE

 A rabbit and a duck went to dinner. Who paid?

The duck—he had the bill.

♥ ♥ ♥ ♥ ♥ ♥ ♥ ♥ ♥ ♥ ♥ ♥

 What did the turtle lying on its back say?
"No, I didn't turn turtle. I've always been one!"

— GEORGE N. NETTO

My sister's children finally got their turn to take home the school's incredibly long-lived guinea pig, Peter. After enjoying his company for a few days, my sister was horrified to find Peter dead one morning. She and her husband hid the cage and dashed to the pet store, intent on replacing the guinea pig before anyone was the wiser.

The pet-store owner listened carefully to their description of Peter's markings. "You're looking for the St. Peter's school guinea pig. I think I have another one," he said calmingly. "You're not the first, you know. Guinea pigs don't live very long."

—CAROL ENGELBERTS

While I was raking leaves along the waterfront of our cottage, I unearthed a fairly large turtle. It appeared to be dead but thinking it might be hibernating, I decided to leave it. Three days later, when it still hadn't moved, I took my rake and gingerly flipped it over. Imagine my surprise when I saw made in china on its underside. I had waited three days for one of my lawn ornaments to move!

Our daughter, a riding instructor, began a lesson with a young girl who was seated on her pony trotting around the school arena.

"How much riding have you done?" she asked the eight-year-old, but there was no answer.

Again, "How much riding have you done?" Still no answer.

In a very loud voice, in case the child was deaf, my daughter bellowed, "How much riding have you done?"

"Oh, sorry," said the girl. "I thought you were talking to my horse."

—LYNN HUGHES

Our two pet bunnies were going to a new home due to the onset of rabbit allergies. Our eight- and five-year-old daughters were sad to see them go. The night after the bunnies went to their new home, my husband told them that he wouldn't be home for lunch the next day because he had to work.

"Oh, great!" said our five-year-old in disgust.

"First the rabbits, now you."

—JEN KUHL

Not the "vet"

The best doctor in the world
is a veterinarian.
He can't ask his patients
what is the matter—
he's got to just know.

—WILL ROGERS

"Who called me a quack?"

❤ ❤ ❤ ❤ ❤ ❤ ❤ ❤ ❤ ❤ ❤

Most of us long for recognition as individuals in our own right, but all too often we are known, as we go through life, as the Jones kid, then Sally Jones' husband, then Johnny Jones' father. But the biggest blow came recently when I visited the vet to pay a bill for our dog.

"Oh, yes," said the secretary when I gave my name, "King's owner!"

—A. B. CALLAWAY

My father-in-law had prostate surgery. We brought him to the hospital at 7:30 a.m., and he was operated on at 8. We were amazed when the hospital called at noon to tell us he could go home. Two months later our beagle, Bo, also had prostate surgery. When I brought him in, I asked the veterinarian what time I should pick him up. The vet told me Bo would remain overnight.

"Overnight?" I said. "My father-in-law came home the same day."

The vet looked at me and said, "Bo's not on Medicare."

—CLYDE DYAR

Concerned, a man took his Rottweiler to the veterinarian. "My dog's cross-eyed," he said. "Is there anything you can do for him?"

"Let's have a look at him," said the vet, lifting the dog up to examine its eyes. "I'm going to have to put him down," he finally said.

"Just because he's cross-eyed?" exclaimed the alarmed pet owner.

"No," said the vet. "Because he's heavy."

—CAO XIN

♥ ♥ ♥ ♥ ♥ ♥ ♥ ♥ ♥ ♥ ♥ ♥

Veterinarian examining cat to cat's owner:
**"I'm afraid we'll have to keep him overnight.
Are you going to need a loaner?"**

—M. TWOHY

I hear plenty of unusual pet names in my job as a veterinarian's assistant. One afternoon I noticed that our next patient was a golden retriever named Brazen.

"I got the idea from my brother," the dog's owner explained when I asked him about the unusual moniker. "His dog is named Shameless. Our last name is Hussey."

—KIRSTEN JOHNSON

While waiting at the veterinarian's office, I overheard two women chatting about their dogs.

"What's your dog's name?" asked the first woman.

"We used to call her Pork Chop," answered the second. "But after all the vet bills we've had for her, we now call her Filet Mignon."

—LAURA SANDERS

It was time for my dog's annual checkup. Following the vet's instructions, I collected a stool sample and dropped it in a plastic container before we left for his office. When we arrived, I handed the sample to the receptionist, who immediately cracked a smile.

The container read: **"I Can't Believe It's Not Butter."**

—MITZI BARNES

♥ ♥ ♥ ♥ ♥ ♥ ♥ ♥ ♥ ♥ ♥

My friend Allison adopted a stray cat and took it to the vet to be neutered.

"I'm about ninety percent certain he's been fixed," the vet said.

"How can I be a hundred percent?" Allison asked.

"Wait to see if he does any 'male' things."

"He already lies on the couch all day," she said. "If he starts hogging the remote, I'll bring him in."

—DORIS MUSICK

When my brother Neill and I were sharing a house, I suggested that he get his pet cat, Speedy, neutered. He agreed but asked me to take Speedy to the veterinarian because his work schedule did not permit him to do so. I dutifully dropped the cat off and was told he would be ready to go home at six o'clock.

Neill was home then, so I told him to go get his cat. To my surprise, he refused and asked me to do it. Annoyed, I demanded that he explain.

Sheepishly, he replied, "I don't want Speedy to know I had anything to do with it."

—AMELIA SCOTT

In his younger days our golden retriever, Catcher, often ran away when he had the chance. His veterinarian's office was about a mile down the road, and Catcher would usually end up there. The office staff knew him well and would call me to come pick him up. One day I called the vet to make an appointment for Catcher's yearly vaccine. "Will you be bringing him?" asked the receptionist. "Or will he be coming on his own?"

—LAURA STASZAK

♥ ♥ ♥ ♥ ♥ ♥ ♥ ♥ ♥ ♥ ♥

A tourist in Maine paid an emergency visit to a veterinarian's office when his dog got the short end of a brawl with a porcupine. After the dog was de-quilled, the man went to pay, but was shocked when the receptionist handed him a bill for $450.

"Four hundred and fifty dollars!" he shouted indignantly. "What do you Mainers do in the wintertime when all the tourists are gone?"

"Raise porcupines," said the receptionist, as she took his check.

—BEATRICE MATHIEU

When our client's dog lapped up anti-freeze, the veterinarian I work for ordered a unique treatment: an IV drip mixing fluids with vodka. "Go buy the cheapest bottle you can find," he told me.

At the liquor store, I was uneasy buying cheap booze so early in the day, and I felt compelled to explain things to the clerk.

"Believe it or not," I said, "this is for a sick dog."

As I was leaving, the next customer plunked down two bottles of muscatel and announced, "These are for my cats."

—DOROTHY SCHOENER

"So...what are you in for?"

❤ ❤ ❤ ❤ ❤ ❤ ❤ ❤ ❤ ❤ ❤

Walking past my father's veterinary clinic, a woman noticed a small boy and his dog waiting outside. "Are you here to see Dr. Meyer?" she asked. "Yes," the boy said. "I'm having my dog put in neutral."

—SALLY MEYER-SHIELDS

Polly the parrot didn't look well, and the vet confirmed it. "I'm sorry," he told the owner, "I'm afraid your bird doesn't have long to live."

"Oh, no," wailed the owner. "Are you sure?"

The vet left the room and returned with a big black Labrador, who sniffed the bird from top to bottom, then shook his head. Next the vet brought in a cat. He too sniffed the parrot and shook his head.

"Your bird is definitely terminal," said the vet, handing the owner a bill.

"Wait—$500! Just to tell me my bird is dying?"

The vet shrugged. "If you'd taken my word for it, the bill would only have been $20, but with the Lab Report and the Cat Scan..."

—DUSTIN GODSEY

Our short-haired collie mix, Toby, was being examined for a cut paw by the veterinarian. "Give me a paw," said the vet. Toby ignored him. "Can he give a paw?" asked the surprised surgeon.

My wife leaned forward and mysteriously replied, "You need to know the right words when there are teenagers in the family."

Then, bending down, she said, "Gimme five, dude," and Toby eagerly held out the wounded paw.

—JIM CLARK

♥ ♥ ♥ ♥ ♥ ♥ ♥ ♥ ♥ ♥ ♥

My mother-in-law's dog was overweight, so the vet gave her some diet pills for the dog. On the return visit the dog's weight was unchanged. The vet asked if she was having trouble getting the dog to take the pills. "Oh no," my mother-in-law answered.

"I hide them in her ice cream!"

—BRENDA SHIPLEY

A man brought in a homing pigeon to a friend of mine who is a veterinarian at an animal hospital. The bird was suffering from an eye infection, and my friend assured the man that treatment would be completed by the next day and the pigeon could be taken home then.

"I'm afraid I'll be out of town tomorrow," the owner replied. "Why not bill me now and let him fly out the window when he's okay?"

—BRUCE LANDESMAN

I was relaxing on the sofa late one evening when I heard my dog crunching something under the table. I lifted the tablecloth, and instead of ruining my favorite shoes, she was devouring my one-month birth-control pill supply.

Worried about the side effects the drug might have on my cherished pet, I phoned the veterinary hot line. With some embarrassment, I explained the situation to the veterinarian on duty, and asked if this "self-medication" could possibly harm my dog.

"Madame, there's absolutely no danger for her," he replied. "But I wouldn't say as much for you!"

—EVELYNE JARRY

♥ ♥ ♥ ♥ ♥ ♥ ♥ ♥ ♥ ♥ ♥

Sign in an animal hospital in Grayslake, Ill.:
"Please do not put pets on counter.
Receptionist bites."

—JEROME BEATTY

Sitting in the vet's waiting room with my dog on my lap, I realized that his tail was slapping the man sitting next to me.

"I'm sorry," I apologized. "There must be a bit of a greyhound in him." Just then the waiting room door opened and a person with a rabbit came in.

"Looks like we're about to find out for sure," commented the man.

—ELIZABETH SIMPSON

"What should I do?" yelled a panicked client to the receptionist at our veterinarian's office. "My dog just ate two bags of unpopped popcorn!" Clearly not as alarmed as the worried pet owner, the receptionist responded coolly, "Well, the first thing I would do is keep him out of the sun."

—BRENDA SHIPLEY

A friend of mine is a deputy with the sheriff's department canine division. One evening, the deputy was dispatched to the scene of a possible burglary, where he discovered the back door of a building ajar. He let the dog out of his patrol car and commanded it to enter and seek. Jumping from the back seat, the dog headed for the building. After lunging through the doorway, the dog froze and backed out. My friend was puzzled until he investigated further. Then he noticed the sign on the building: "Veterinarian's office."

—ELIZABETH BENNETT

QUOTABLE QUOTES

"First I wanted to be a veterinarian. And then I realized you had to give them shots to put them to sleep, so I decided I'd just buy a bunch of animals and have them in my house instead."

—PARIS HILTON

"Of all the things I miss from veterinary practice, puppy breath is one of the most fond memories!"

—DR. TOM CAT

"We can judge the heart of a man by his treatment of animals."

—IMMANUEL KANT

"I had planned to retire when I was 13...I had wanted to be a veterinarian."

—LINDA BLAIR

"Everything I know I learned from my cat: When you're hungry, eat. When you're tired, nap in a sunbeam. When you go to the vet's, pee on your owner."

—GARY SMITH

"A man who carries a cat by the tail learns something he can learn in no other way."

—MARK TWAIN

"A piece of grass a day keeps the vet away."

—UNKNOWN DOG

"Outside of a dog, a book is man's best friend. Inside a dog, it's too dark to read."

—GROUCHO MARX

♥ ♥ ♥ ♥ ♥ ♥ ♥ ♥ ♥ ♥ ♥

One day at the veterinarian's office where I take my cat, a man and the receptionist were verbally sparring. After a few moments a technician came to her coworker's defense. "Sir," she interjected, "do you know what happens to aggressive males in this office?"

—VIVIANE HUESTIS

Like most puppies, mine is not finicky about what he puts in his mouth; he eats anything. But the day he swallowed a quarter, I panicked and called the vet. "What should I do?" I pleaded over the phone.

My extremely laid-back vet answered calmly, "Swallowing a quarter is nothing to worry about. But if he does it again and a can of Pepsi shoots out of his rear, give me a call."

—SUSAN GORBY

A client recently brought her two cats to my husband's veterinary clinic for their annual checkup. One was a small-framed, round tiger-striped tabby, while the other was a long, sleek black cat.

She watched closely as I put each on the scale. "They weigh about the same," I told her.

"That proves it!" she exclaimed. "Black does make you look slimmer. And stripes make you look fat."

—SUSAN DANIEL

 Why did the snail take off his shell?
He was feeling a little sluggish.

— KEITH JOHNS

"Well, I'd say it's from too many years of being patted on the head."

♥ ♥ ♥ ♥ ♥ ♥ ♥ ♥ ♥ ♥ ♥

I heard the dog barking before he and his owner actually barreled into our vet practice. Spotting a training video we sell, the owner wisely decided to buy one.

"How does this work?" she asked, handing me a check. **"Do I just have him watch this?"**

—BRANDI CHYTKA

When she got back to her rural home after participating in an animal rights march in Washington, D.C., my friend Joan let her pet cat out into the yard. Twenty minutes later she was shocked to find the cat returning with a baby rabbit in its mouth. Removing the rabbit, Joan placed it in a box, grabbed her car keys, and headed for the animal shelter. On the way, she accidentally hit a squirrel. She stopped the car, put the squirrel in the box and went on to the shelter. There, a wildlife worker told Joan that he could do nothing for the animals.

"But I'm glad you brought them in," he said, "now we can feed the owl."

—FRANK MALANDRA

Our grandson has a pet rabbit named Wabbit. One day David came home from school and found that Wabbit had injured a front foot and couldn't walk. He was rushed to the veterinary clinic. After examining Wabbit, the vet returned him to the front desk. Entered on his medical chart was this diagnosis: "Wabbit Gilbert. Wist not bwoken, onwy spwained. Spwint not necessawy."

—ESTHER GILBERT

♥ ♥ ♥ ♥ ♥ ♥ ♥ ♥ ♥ ♥ ♥

There was no way we were giving up the stray kitten who adopted us. We called her Princess. When we took her to the animal hospital to get her checked out, the vet had news: She was actually a he. "So what's the new name going to be?" he asked. "The Cat Formerly Known as Princess?"

—JEANETTE ANDERSON

My five-year-old daughter, Rahne, and I had been discussing what people eat and how some people choose to be vegetarian. About a week later, Rahne was talking about what she wanted to be when she grew up. "It would be great to be a veterinarian," she said, "but I wouldn't want to stop eating bacon."

—ANGELA TEMPLETON

As a veterinarian, I was called at home in the middle of the night by a woman in distress. She had swallowed her dog's heart-worm pill by mistake. I knew it wouldn't harm her, but by law, I'm forbidden to give medical advice.

"If your dog had swallowed your pill, then you'd call me," I explained. "In this case, you really should consult with your own physician."

"But it's one in the morning!" she exclaimed,

"I can't wake my doctor."

—CHERYL SACKLER

"Please stick out your tongue again, only much, much, much slower."

♥ ♥ ♥ ♥ ♥ ♥ ♥ ♥ ♥ ♥ ♥

Veterinarian to cat owner:
**"Give him one of these pills every four hours.
Then use this to stop your bleeding."**

—GEORGE WOLFE

Our veterinarian gave us the following instructions for our cat, Friday, who was scheduled for surgery: "Don't give Friday any food after 8 p.m. on Wednesday. Bring Friday in first thing Thursday morning. You can pick him up Thursday evening. But if you want, Friday can also stay until Friday."

—MARY MALLOY

A woman walked into my aunt's animal shelter wanting to have her cat and six kittens spayed and neutered.

"Is the mother friendly?" my aunt asked.

"Very," said the woman, casting an eye on all the pet carriers.

"That's how we got into this mess in the first place."

—SARAH MITCHELL

A new client brought his poodle to my office. As I approached the dog, it growled. "How is he with veterinarians?" I asked.

"Oh, fine!" The owner responded jovially, "He hasn't bitten one yet!"

Reassured by this, I began my examination. Suddenly, before I could react, the dog turned and bit my hand. "I thought you said he'd never bitten a veterinarian!" I exclaimed.

"He hadn't," the owner replied. "until now they've all been fast enough."

—R. SNOPEK

♥ ♥ ♥ ♥ ♥ ♥ ♥ ♥ ♥ ♥ ♥

A woman telephoned a veterinarian and asked him to come examine her cat.

"I don't know what's wrong with her," the woman told him. "She looks as if she's going to have kittens, but that's impossible. She's never been out of the house except when I had her on a leash."

The vet examined the cat and said there was no doubt of her pregnancy.

"But she can't be," protested her mistress. "It's impossible."

At that point a large tom cat emerged from under the sofa.

"How about him?" the vet asked.

"Don't be silly," said the woman. "That's her brother!"

—R.K. CLIFTON

Higgins, our dog, was sick throughout the weekend, so first thing Monday my wife, Hildy, took him to the vet. The doctor prescribed antibiotics and suggested Higgins be given just small amounts of food. Soon after, Hildy called me at the office before she left for work to explain when to give the antibiotics and what to feed him. "I'm cooking rice and hamburger meat for the dog now," she told me.

"How nice," I said. "What about me?"

"Don't worry," she replied. "You can have some, too."

—PAT BATTISTA

On a visit to the veterinarian with our schnauzer, my mother saw a post card on the bulletin board: "Dear Buffy, we are having a wonderful vacation. Hope you are enjoying your stay with Dr. McAfee and being a good dog. Next year you can come with us, and the kids will stay with Dr. McAfee."

—DENNA C. GLEASON

♥ ♥ ♥ ♥ ♥ ♥ ♥ ♥ ♥ ♥ ♥

In my house we always treated our pets as if they were members of the family. Our dog, Lord, occupies a privileged position. One Saturday morning the telephone rang and, when I answered it, I heard a female voice on the other end.

"Good morning! Is this the Lord Gonçalves house?"

It was the veterinarian calling to change the time of Lord's appointment to have his coat clipped.

—MARIA FERNANDA GONÇALVES

In the waiting room of our local vet's surgery, an elderly woman sitting opposite me patted my pup and asked what kind of dog it was.

"He's a border terrier," I said proudly. "Oh, so is mine," she replied.

"Is it?" I said with surprise, looking at the ancient mongrel at her feet.

"Yes," she continued. "He's on the borders of a terrier, a Labrador and a sheepdog."

—ELIZABETH ANN CROPPER

My son, Isaac, had had a number of operations by the time he was 4 years old and had become quite matter-of-fact about them.

One day when we were at the veterinarian's office for our new kitten's checkup, Isaac suddenly looked up from the toys he was playing with and seemed to notice his surroundings for the first time. **"Mom,"** he asked in a room full of people holding their pets, **"am I here to be fixed?"**

—CAROLE NICHOLSON

♥ ♥ ♥ ♥ ♥ ♥ ♥ ♥ ♥ ♥ ♥

Seen in the Pets section of the yellow pages:
"Spading and Neutering. **We treat your pets like family."**

—TIRZAH CARROLL

My husband, an accountant, is allergic to cats, so when he was on an assignment at a veterinarian's office, he made sure there'd be no cats in residence that day. However, he soon started to sneeze and his eyes began to water. The receptionist, who was sitting in the same office, assured Ian that there were no cats present.

A miserable half hour later, he couldn't stand it any longer and decided to finish the work at his own office. As he was packing up to leave, he remarked how odd it was for him to be having a reaction. The receptionist then reached under her desk and pulled out a box. "Well," she said, "we don't have any cats here today, but we do have this litter of kittens."

—R. J. HUTCHINSON

One of our clients brought in his massive pinscher to be spayed. As a veterinary assistant, I escort the patient into the doctor's office. But before taking this dog's leash, I glimpsed those large teeth of hers and asked the owner, "Is she friendly?" "Friendly?" said the man. "She's had five litters!"

—JUNE GOUVAS

As part of a ranching family, our daughters are constantly around animals. This explained the conversation at dinner one night when our six-year-old announced, "I never want to have children."

"Then you'll have to go to the vet," our four-year-old declared.

—KATHARINE HELLER

"I hope your temperature is normal too— like Spots was."

♥ ♥ ♥ ♥ ♥ ♥ ♥ ♥ ♥ ♥ ♥

A stockman fell off his horse and broke his leg out in the bush. The horse grabbed the stockman's belt in his teeth, dragged him to shelter, then went to fetch the doctor. Discussing the incident a few weeks later, a friend praised the horse's intelligence. "He's not that smart," replied the stockman. "He came back with the vet!"

—J. WHALLEY

I got my strangest job from a man who was taking care of a puppy for a journalist friend on assignment overseas. He came to me with the dog in one hand and a tape recorder in the other. He told me that the usually docile puppy cried, soiled the carpets, chewed furniture and tore pillows to shreds in its new home, and he had been at a loss to understand why. That is, until he talked to a veterinarian. The doctor explained that the puppy was upset because it missed the constant clatter of the journalist's typewriter. I was hired to tape-record two hours of continuous typing, to be played for the puppy whenever it got restless. It worked.

—JILL K. NEMIROW

A man walked into the vet's office and asked to have his dog's tail removed. Having expressed his reluctance to perform the operation unless it was completely necessary, asked the dog-owner why he wanted this service performed.

"Well," replied the man, **"my mother-in-law is coming to stay, and I don't want her to see any sign of a welcome."**

—DAVID MACRAE

♥ ♥ ♥ ♥ ♥ ♥ ♥ ♥ ♥ ♥ ♥

Feeling horrible, an alligator goes to the veterinarian.

"What seems to be the problem?" the vet asks.

"I just don't have the drive I used to, doc," the gator says. "Used to be, I could swim underwater for miles and catch any animal I wanted. Now all I can do is let them swim by." Concerned, the vet gives him a thorough examination and hands him a few pills.

"What are these?" the gator asks.

"It's a pill very similar to Viagra," the vet answers.

"Hold on, I don't have that kind of problem," the alligator protests. "What exactly is wrong with me?"

"Well," the vet said, "you have a reptile disfunction."

—MICHAEL SULLIVAN

A veterinarian who works in the same building as I do told me about a young man who had stopped by his clinic earlier that day. "Doc," the man said, "I've got a problem. My buddy gave me a Rottweiler as a present." The man paused.

"Yes," my friend prompted, "but that wouldn't seem to me to be much of a problem."

"You wouldn't say that," the man said, "if it was you who couldn't get back into his own house!"

—BOB JOHNSON

One day at the animal hospital where I worked, an owner brought an African grey parrot in to have its beak and wings trimmed. The owner warned that the parrot disliked these procedures and was apt to bite. I donned thick gloves and cautiously opened the cage. The parrot stepped out and, looking up at me, said, "Don't worry, I won't hurt you."

—MICHELE SERVIDEO

"With this type of condition, it doesn't hurt to be extra careful."

♥ ♥ ♥ ♥ ♥ ♥ ♥ ♥ ♥ ♥ ♥

One day, my daughter came home from school with a kitten in her arms. The poor creature had a limp, but we couldn't keep it, so we decided to take it to the vet's to have it seen to. The diagnostic was disappointment; the leg was broken, and the vet suggested putting the animal down. When I told my daughter what that meant, her reaction was overwhelming: It's all very well for you grown-ups. But what difference does it make to have a painless death once you're dead? And she burst into tears. That night, the kitten slept in her room.

—L. P.

Our vet was called out of his bed at 2:30 A.M. by a taxi driver who had run over a cat. The vet said there was no hope for it and, in consultation with the taxi driver, decided to put it to sleep for good.

"How much do I owe you?" asked the taxi driver.

"Nothing." said the vet. "You came to me even though you really hadn't the time. I just did my duty. That cat must be in heaven by now, so I'll send the bill to our Lord."

Late that morning a box of chocolates was delivered to the vet. In unpracticed writing stood: "With my thanks for the return of my black cat. Yours respectfully, O. Lord."

—H. O.

Caitlyn, our four-year-old niece, lived on a farm and was watching her dad and the vet work with some cattle. When the vet's hat fell off, she jumped down and picked it up but continued searching for something.

Finally, she handed the bald vet his hat saying, "Here's your hat, but I couldn't find your hair."

—BONI SCHILTROTH

❤ ❤ ❤ ❤ ❤ ❤ ❤ ❤ ❤ ❤ ❤

On a busy morning a veterinarian received a call from a woman who said she was starting a poultry farm and wanted to know how long she should leave the rooster with the hens.

"Just a minute," replied the vet as his other phone rang.

"Thank you very much," said the woman, and hung up.

My cat always struggles as if possessed whenever we have to hold her—even if it's only to trim her claws. Naturally, we were apprehensive when the time came to bring her to the veterinarian. During the examination, I commented, "I sure would hate to be the vet who's going to give her an injection."

"I'd hate even more to be the owner who's going to hold her," the vet replied swiftly.

—CARMEN LANDRY

I told my 11-year-old daughter to telephone the pet store when the hamster we had bought there an hour earlier started chewing feverishly on its leg. She was told the hamster should be taken to a veterinarian right away. I was outraged, knowing the bill for the vet would be greater than the cost of the hamster, so I asked Ali to call the pet store again and hand the phone to me.

"Were you just speaking to my daughter about her sick hamster?" I asked.

"Yes," came the reply.

"Have you any idea how expensive a visit to the vet will be?" I ranted. "You had better either replace the hamster or pay the vet bill!" I demanded.

"Gee, ma'am," came the meek reply, "we're just a television repair store."

—BARBARA RODEN

♥ ♥ ♥ ♥ ♥ ♥ ♥ ♥ ♥ ♥ ♥ ♥

My sister's dog was ill and in need of a veterinarian when we arrived at her house for a visit. After being told by her aunt that a vet was a dog doctor, my four-year-old daughter wanted to accompany them to his office. When the doctor was introduced to her, she looked accusingly at her aunt and declared, **"He's not a dog!"**

—MARGARET ROOT

Working for a veterinarian on a hectic Saturday morning, I picked up the ringing phone and was asked, "How much does it cost to get a dog fixed?"

Not knowing if the pet was male or female, I inquired, "Do you mean neutered or spayed?"

To which she answered, "Whichever is cheapest."

—JEAN KERN

A man had a horse that some days trotted friskily and other days limped. Concerned, he decided to take it to the vet.

"Doctor, I have a horse that sometimes walks well and sometimes limps," he said. "What should I do?"

The vet replied with hesitation: "Well, sell it on a day when it walks well, and you've got yourself a good deal!"

—LUIS FERNANDO ORDOÑEZ

A small town's sheriff was also its lone veterinarian. One night, the phone rang and his wife answered. "Let me speak to your husband!" a voice demanded. "Do you require his services as a sheriff or a vet?" the wife asked. "Both," cried the caller. "We can't get our dog's mouth open and there's a burglar in it."

Dumb *and* dumber

I gave my cat a bath the other day...he loved it. He sat there, he enjoyed it, it was fun for me. The fur would stick to my tongue, but other than that...

—STEVE MARTIN

"So, we'll give him a bone
and which ever end eats it is the front."

♥ ♥ ♥ ♥ ♥ ♥ ♥ ♥ ♥ ♥

"How do you spell toad?" one of my first-grade students asked.

"We just read a story about a toad," I said, then helped him spell it out: "T-O-A-D."

Satisfied, he finished writing the story he'd begun, then read it aloud: "I toad my mama I wanted a dog for my birthday."

—JOANNA POTTER

It was our cat's first winter. When a raging blizzard came up suddenly, we tried frantically to find Ginger, calling him repeatedly and poking into snowdrifts around the stoop where he liked to hide. Finally I called the police station to inquire if a "found" cat had been reported. The sergeant listened politely to my concerns and assured me that cats had been known to live through terrible storms.

"Ginger," I added, on a hopeful note, "is exceptionally intelligent. In fact, he almost talks."

"In that case, lady," replied the officer, "hang up. He's probably trying to call you now."

—FLORENCE MCGILTON

I work for an insurance brokerage firm that places unusual risks many underwriters will not assume. One day I had two such requests, so I called Lloyd's of London. Would they insure a show cat for an airplane trip, and would they insure a parrot against any physical harm?

There was a pause, and then a woman responded in a clipped British accent, "Yes, we can insure a bird, or we can insure a cat, but certainly not the both together."

—TOMMY GREIG

♥ ♥ ♥ ♥ ♥ ♥ ♥ ♥ ♥ ♥ ♥

When my husband wanted me to accompany him on a business trip of several months, I couldn't bear the thought of putting our old dog in a kennel for so long.

"We'll take him with us," said my husband. "There must be at least one hotel in every city that will take pets."

But in one Texas city our directory did not list a single hotel that accepted dogs.

"I'll write for reservations anyhow," said my husband.

A few days later we received a reply saying that our party would be most welcome.

"What did you say to get such an answer?" I exclaimed. He handed me a carbon of his letter. It was a routine request for reservations, except for this closing sentence: "And would you mind if we bring along an elderly refined old gentleman, who happens to be a dog?"

—VIRGINIA O'FARRELL

A customer at the pet-food store where I work went to the bulk flavor-treat bin and picked out all the green and red bone-shaped biscuits. There weren't enough, so I opened another box and asked if her dog liked only those flavors.

"Oh, no," she replied. "I'm making him a Christmas wreath."

—NICOLA NEWTON

Here's a tip: Make sure your wife knows you're talking to a cat under her chair begging for food before you say,
"You know you're already twice as fat as you should be."

—ROBERT ESPOSITO

♥ ♥ ♥ ♥ ♥ ♥ ♥ ♥ ♥ ♥ ♥

We visited our newly married daughter, who was preparing her first Thanksgiving dinner. I noticed the turkey thawing in the kitchen sink with a dish drainer inverted over the bird. I asked why a drainer covered the turkey. Our daughter turned to my wife and said, "Mom, you always did it that way."

"Yes," my wife replied, "but you don't have a cat!"

—A. C. STOKE, JR.

Several neighbors had gathered for dinner, and the conversation turned to pets. Our hostess commented that she had the dumbest dog ever. "Any dog that digs up the same rose bush twenty times has to be pretty dumb," she said.

Everyone seemed to agree, until the 75-year-old grandmother of the neighborhood remarked, "I'm not too surprised at the dog, but I am a little concerned about the person who planted the rose bush that many times"

—RUTH MADDOX

Department stores were holding "white sales," and I decided to go shopping with my children, telling them they could choose one item that had been reduced. I expected them to head immediately for the bargain table at the toy store. The children ran off. A few minutes later they returned and excitedly dragged me past the toy store and toward a pet shop whose owner was holding a small black dog with a large white spot under its chin. The sign in the pet store window read: "'White sale.' All animals with white on them will be marked down 15%."

The children got their dog.

—CARREN STROCK

❤ ❤ ❤ ❤ ❤ ❤ ❤ ❤ ❤ ❤ ❤

Printed on the back of a bottle of dog shampoo:
"Cruelty free—not tested on animals."

—WALT BAZELLA

A couple had just moved into a new home. As they were preparing for bed one night, their cat, Mister, started begging to go out. The couple hesitated because they wondered if the cat had become familiar with the new surroundings yet. But the cat kept insisting, and the couple finally decided to let him go.

When the wife awoke at daybreak, she remembered that Mister was still out, so she crept out of bed and tiptoed to the front door.

"Mister, Mister," she called softly. No cat. She stepped outside and called louder, "Mister! Mister! Don't you want to come in?" That time the cat heard her—and so did a jogger running in front of her house. The cat streaked inside and the jogger called back, "No, thank you, ma'am—not this morning."

—GEORGE DOLAN

I work for an allergist, and one frequent patient is a mailman who will often regale me with his on-the-job stories. A homeowner on his new route has a Doberman pinscher that is left outside in the fenced-in front yard, where the mailbox is located. In an excited voice, the mailman told me that he barely made it through the gate when the large dog lunged at him.

"I've decided that I won't make any more deliveries to that house until they put the mailbox outside the fence," he declared.

"How will you notify them about that?" I asked.

"Oh," he answered without thinking. "That's easy. We'll just send them a letter."

—KATE WARNER

♥ ♥ ♥ ♥ ♥ ♥ ♥ ♥ ♥ ♥ ♥

John disliked the family cat, and decided
to get rid of him. He drove the feline 20 blocks
from home and left him. But when he pulled
into his driveway, there was the cat.
The next day he left the kitty 40 blocks away,
but again, the cat beat him home.

So he took the cat on a long drive, arbitrarily
turning left, then right, making U-turns, anything to
throw off the tabby's keen sense of direction before
abandoning him in a park across town.

Hours later John called his wife: "Jen, is the cat there?"

"Yes," she replied. "Why?"

"Put him on the phone. I'm lost and need directions home."

♥ ♥ ♥ ♥ ♥ ♥ ♥ ♥ ♥ ♥

My aunt's neighbor in New York had a beautiful black cat, Villiam, who spent his days outside and came indoors at night. One cool October evening, he disappeared. The neighbor searched for him in vain.

The following spring, however, Villiam reappeared, looking healthy and clean. She figured he'd been sowing his wild oats. Everything was back to normal, until that autumn, when Villiam disappeared again. The next spring, he returned. Perplexed, my aunt's friend began asking neighbors for clues.

Finally she rang the bell of an older couple. "A black cat?" the woman said. "Oh, yes. My husband and I hated to see him out in the cold, so we bought a cat carrier. We take him to Florida every winter."

—NORMA TREADWELL

A dog walks into a telegram office, takes out a blank form and writes, "Woof. Woof. Woof. Woof. Woof. Woof. Woof. Woof. Woof."

"There are only nine words here," says the clerk. "You could send another 'woof' for the same price."

The dog looks at him, confused. "But that wouldn't make any sense."

A customer called our florist shop to order a bouquet. "Make it bright and festive looking," she said. **"I want it to cheer up a friend. She just lost her Seeing Eye dog."**

—KATHY BRENING

♥ ♥ ♥ ♥ ♥ ♥ ♥ ♥ ♥ ♥ ♥

After new neighbors moved in, our garbage was knocked over in the mornings by their big black dog. I'd often try to shoo him away, but he'd only snarl at me. In exasperation, I went to my neighbors to complain.

"Thank you for telling me," said the woman who opened the door. "We noticed he had bad breath, but we didn't know where he was getting it."

—JEANNE WATKO

Veterinarian Louis J. Camuti used to tell of one of his more unusual house calls: My client, Mrs. Rouben Mamoulian, wife of the stage-and-screen director, lived a life of luxury. Her cat, however, was an ordinary gray tabby named Dinah. Or so I thought. Actually, I found out that Dinah was the cat's meow when Mrs. Mamoulian one day asked, "Would you like to see her wardrobe?"

She led the way to a room dominated by a large French armoire. Holding up several tiny outfits, she asked, "Aren't they fine?"

"But your cat wasn't wearing anything when I saw her just now."

Mrs. Mamoulian looked at me as if I were a fool and said, "Of course not. The cat isn't going anywhere."

She kept pulling out more and more cat-size garments: gowns, petticoats, a cape.

"It's incredible," I exclaimed, "these clothes look tailor-made."

"Well, of course they are," she replied, giving me a scorching look. "How else could we get a decent fit?"

—MARILYN AND HASKEL FRANKEL

QUOTABLE QUOTES

"My new horse was sold to me as a real gentleman to ride. He is. When we have to go over a fence, he insists on 'ladies first.'"

—ANONYMOUS

"I've got a new invention. It's a revolving bowl for tired goldfish."

—LEFTY GOMEZ

"We've begun to long for the pitter-patter of little feet—so we bought a dog. Well, it's cheaper, and you get more feet."

—RITA RUDNER

"A dog teaches a boy fidelity, perseverance, and to turn around three times before lying down."

—ROBERT BENCHLEY

"Man is rated the highest animal, at least among all animals who returned the questionnaire."

—ROBERT BRAULT

"To ride or not to ride—this is a stupid question."

—BRANDY MICHELLE

"Be the person your dog thinks you are."

—UNKNOWN

"Relax. I just had a cappuccino."

♥ ♥ ♥ ♥ ♥ ♥ ♥ ♥ ♥ ♥ ♥

Two brothers, Herbert and James, lived with their mother and a cat named Edgar. James was particularly attached to the cat, and when he had to leave town for several days, he left Herbert meticulous instructions about the pet's care. At the end of his first day away, James telephoned his brother. "How is Edgar?" he asked.

"Edgar is dead," Herbert answered. There was a pause. Then James said, "Herbert, you're insensitive. You know how close I was to Edgar—you should have broken the news to me slowly. When I asked about Edgar tonight, you should have said, 'Edgar's on the roof, but I've called the fire department to get him down.' And tomorrow when I called, you could have said the firemen were having trouble getting Edgar down, but you were hopeful they would succeed. Then when I called the third time, you could have told me that the firemen had done their best, but unfortunately Edgar had fallen off the roof and was at the veterinarian's. Then when I called the last time, you could have said that although everything possible had been done for Edgar, he had died. That's the way a sensitive man would have told me about Edgar. And, oh, before I forget," James added, "how is mother?"

"Uh," Herbert said, pausing for a moment, "she's on the roof."

—SAMUEL F. PICKERING

What did the airhead name her pet zebra?
Spot

♥ ♥ ♥ ♥ ♥ ♥ ♥ ♥ ♥ ♥

I had an inauspicious start as a dog groomer when one of my first clients bit me. Noticing my pain, my boss voiced her concern. **"Whatever you do,"** she said, **"don't bleed on the white dogs."**

—JAN VIRGO

A fellow salesperson, an animal lover, was suddenly overcome by allergies at one of our company meetings. Coughing, sniffling, watery eyes...she was a mess.

"If you have such terrible allergies, why do you keep so many pets?" asked a friend.

"Because"—sneeze, cough, hack—"if I'm going to be sick, I might as well have company."

—JOHN CALDWELL

Two friends run into each other while walking their dogs. One suggests lunch. The other says, "They won't let us in a restaurant with pets." Undeterred, the first guy and his German shepherd head into the restaurant. The maitre d' stops them, saying, "Sir, you can't bring your dog in here."

"But I'm blind," the man replies, "and this is my guide dog." The maitre d', apologizing profusely, shows both man and dog to a table. His friend waits five minutes, then tries the same routine.

"You have a chihuahua for a guide dog?" the skeptical maitre d' says.

"A chihuahua?" the man says. "Is that what they gave me?"

—MORT SHEINMAN

♥ ♥ ♥ ♥ ♥ ♥ ♥ ♥ ♥ ♥

On the beach, a poacher was stopped by a game warden who said he'd be fined for taking lobsters without a permit.

"What do you mean?" the man said, "I didn't break the law. These two lobsters are my pets. I'm just going for a walk with them."

"Nonsense," the game warden replied.

"It's true," said the man. "They go into the surf for a swim, and when I whistle they come back to me."

"This I've got to see," the game warden said.

So the man tossed both of the lobsters out into the waves and the game warden said, "Okay. Now let's hear you whistle for your pet lobsters to swim back to you."

"Lobsters?" asked the poacher. "What lobsters?"

—THE JOKESMITH

My sight-impaired friend was in a grocery store with her guide dog when the manager asked, "Is that a blind dog?"

My friend said, "I hope not, or we're both in trouble."

—SUE YOUNG

Each year, the pet shop where I work participates in a parade with other stores located in the same strip mall. The pet-shop owner "volunteers" a friend to march in costume as Blue Kitty and then to walk through the mall greeting shoppers and their children.

After one parade, Blue Kitty came racing through the store and disappeared into the back room. I followed, somewhat perplexed. When I reached Blue Kitty, he was frantically trying to remove the costume.

"Boy, is this a problem," he said, "I have to use the litter box."

—M. C. WEIMAN

♥ ♥ ♥ ♥ ♥ ♥ ♥ ♥ ♥ ♥ ♥

My sister adopted a scraggly black puppy just before she was to catch a flight from Kansas to Florida. She immediately made special arrangements with the airline to take her new pet on the plane. At the Kansas City airport my sister prepared to board, puppy in a carrying case tucked under her arm. To the amusement of fellow travelers, she was wearing a t-shirt that read: "Dear Auntie Em, hate the farm, hate Kansas, taking the dog.—Dorothy."

—CINDY VOIGT

I was given a kitten by a coworker, and we went to a snack bar to find a box for the trip home. One labeled "chocolate raisins" seemed perfect. I put my new pet in it, loosely fastened the top and headed for the building elevator.

A young marine in full dress uniform—obviously about to go on duty at the nearby White House complex—entered the elevator with me. To my embarrassment, the kitten began trying to get out of its box, scratching and mewing furiously. The Marine stood ramrod straight, looking neither to the right nor left.

"Ma'am," he stated with finality, "your raisins are trying to escape."

—VANNA J. SHIELDS

Police officers in Brockton, Massachusetts, received a call regarding an injured animal lying on a street corner. When they arrived at the scene, they found a dog that had been hit by a car. But according to the *Brockton Enterprise,* the police report stated that the dog was okay and "refused medical treatment."

—ELEANOR CLAFF

"Let me show you what you're doing wrong."

♥ ♥ ♥ ♥ ♥ ♥ ♥ ♥ ♥ ♥ ♥

Spotted outside a veterinary hospital in Clinton, Utah:
"Happy Father's Day! Neutering Special."

—SHARON NAUTA STEELE

Our local newspaper, *The DeSoto Appeal,* runs a popular column called "10 Questions" that spotlights people who live in our community. In addition to the usual inquiries about occupation and age, people are asked the questions that give a snapshot of their personalities. Recently, one woman was asked, "What's the strangest thing you ever bought?" She answered, "Dog toothpaste." Next question: "What is the most common thing people say to you?" Answer: "Where did you get your white teeth?"

—JACKIE HANNAMAN

Parking on a hill near a supermarket, a woman got out of her car, locked the door and gave a parting command to her dog, who was lying low on the rear seat.

"Stay!" she said loudly.

Unable to see the dog, a bystander watched with amused interest. "Hey," he called out. "Why don't you try putting on the emergency brake?"

—J. M. STEWART

I went looking for a restroom and found two doors with pictures of dogs on them. I was completely baffled, so I searched out the manager and admitted I couldn't tell the difference between the male dog and the female dog. The manager smiled and said, "That's not the idea. One dog is a pointer, the other a setter."

—EDWARD D. GRIMES

❤ ❤ ❤ ❤ ❤ ❤ ❤ ❤ ❤ ❤

As I drove into a parking lot, I noticed that a pickup truck with a dog sitting behind the wheel was rolling toward a female pedestrian. She seemed oblivious, so I hit my horn to get her attention. She looked up just in time to jump out of the truck's path, and the vehicle bumped harmlessly into the curb and stopped.

I rushed to the woman's side to see if she was all right. "Thanks, I'm fine," she assured me, "but if that dog hadn't honked..."

—PEGGY GREENWOOD

My uncle lives alone with a menagerie of animals—dogs, cats, rabbits and goats. One day, I was visiting and found a note stuck to the door, which read, "The dogs ate Boo Boo."

Knowing how my uncle felt about his pets, I frantically searched the yard for Boo Boo's remains, but found nothing. "Sorry to hear about Boo Boo," I said to my uncle later, as I showed him the note. "Which one was he?"

My uncle read the note, and then grinned. "Boo Boo's my neighbor. He means he fed the dogs."

—MARTHA CARROLL

After yet another toilet-bowl funeral for a pet goldfish, my three-year-old granddaughter, Harper, was telling her mom how sad it was to have all her pets die. My daughter agreed, and added, "At least they're in heaven."

"Heaven's in the toilet?" Harper asked.

—PAM YEMEN

"I guess I won't wear the bonnet."

♥ ♥ ♥ ♥ ♥ ♥ ♥ ♥ ♥ ♥ ♥

A guy spots a sign outside a house that reads "Talking Dog for Sale." Intrigued, he walks in.

"So what have you done with your life?" he asks the dog.

"I've led a very full life," says the dog. "I lived in the Alps rescuing avalanche victims. Then I served my country in Iraq. And now I spend my days reading to the residents of a retirement home."

The guy is flabbergasted. He asks the dog's owner, "Why on earth would you want to get rid of an incredible dog like that?"

The owner says, "Because he's a liar! He never did any of that!"

—HARRY NELSON

A man and his dog go to a movie. During the funny scenes, the dog laughs. When there's a sad part, the dog cries. This goes on for the entire film: laughing and crying in all the right places. After the show, a man who was sitting in the row behind them comes up and says, "That was truly amazing!"

"It sure was," the dog owner replies. "He hated the book."

—DONALD GEISER

Entering a friend's home for his weekly poker game, Slick is amazed to see a dog sitting at the table. He's even more surprised when the dog wins the first hand with a full house, and takes the second with a royal flush.

"This is unreal," Slick says after the dog wins the next two hands "He's got to be the only dog in the world that can play like that."

"Aw, he's not so great," says the host. "There's a dog in Vegas who doesn't wag his tail every time he gets a good hand."

At first it was funny. Whenever our mother played the piano, our poodle would sing along—enthusiastically, in an earsplitting howl. We would all laugh, but after a while, my dad couldn't take it any longer. "For Pete's sake," he begged, "play something the dog doesn't know."

—TEMPLE LYMBERIS

The week we got our puppy, I caught a stomach bug and stayed home from work one day. That afternoon, my wife called to check up on me.

"I'm okay," I said. "But guess who pooped in the dining room."

My wife's response: "Who?"

—RUSSELL MOORE

One afternoon I was walking on a trail with my newborn daughter, chatting to her about the scenery. When a man and his dog approached, I leaned into the baby carriage and said, "See the doggy?"

Suddenly I felt a little silly talking to my baby as if she understood me. But just as the man passed, I noticed he reached down, patted his dog and said, "See the baby?"

—CATHERINE REARDON

A woman at my friend's pet shop pointed to a Labrador puppy. "I want that one," she said. **"But I don't want the floor model."**

—CINTHIA GAGNON

 Where do you find a dog with no legs?
Exactly where you left it.

— KEITH JOHNS

One morning while a locksmith had come to change the locks in my house, I realized I had to run a few errands. I turned to him, a sweet older man, and said I was heading out. As I got to the front door, I noticed my sad-faced dog staring at me from the living room.

"I love you, sweet boy," I said. "Now you be good. Okay?"

From the other room I heard a voice answer, "Okay."

—ANGELA MILLER

When my friend spotted a blind man and his guide dog at a crosswalk, she stopped her car and waved them on.

"Uh, Cynthia," I said, "he can't see you."

"I know that," she said indignantly. "I'm waving the dog on."

—CAREN FORREST

Enclosed with the heartworm pills my friend received from a veterinarian was a sheet of red heart stickers to place on a calendar as a reminder to give her pet the medication. She attached these stickers to her kitchen calendar, marking the first Saturday of every month. When her husband noticed the hearts, he grinned from ear to ear, turned to his wife and asked, "Do you have something special in mind for these days?"

—MARY LOUISE RUSSO

♥ ♥ ♥ ♥ ♥ ♥ ♥ ♥ ♥ ♥ ♥

In an upscale pet-supply store, a customer wanted to buy a red sweater for her dog. The clerk suggested that she bring her dog in for a proper fit.

"I can't do that!" she said. **"The sweater is going to be a surprise!"**

—HAROLD M. JOHNSEN

After buying our new home, we landscaped it. Since this was my husband's first attempt at planting a lawn, he was careful to do the job right. He prepared the soil, put in a sprinkler system and waited. Finally, after work on a day when the weather was exactly right, he seeded the lawn, rolled it and watered it—finishing by artificial light because it got so late.

For the next three weeks he watered the lawn daily, often rushing home at noon to run the sprinklers for an hour. He fussed over it, shooed away birds and our cat, and looked for the first blade of grass to peek through. Except for a few weeds, nothing happened. Then one Saturday morning my husband came in and announced sheepishly, "I just found the sack of grass seed in the garage."

"What in the world did you plant?" I asked.

With a sigh he replied, "Kitty litter."

—RUTH N. KOHL

While in San Antonio, Texas, my wife and I decided to visit the zoo, and I called ahead to ask if it would be all right to bring our pet. The woman I spoke to answered sternly, "We don't allow animals in the zoo."

—JOHN DEFRONZO

"You're really quite mad."

❤ ❤ ❤ ❤ ❤ ❤ ❤ ❤ ❤ ❤

Doctor holding cat above his patient's head:
"I'm just going to give you a cat scan."

In a hurry to deliver her cupcakes to the school bake sale, my sister JoAnn went to her storage area and quickly grabbed the lid to an old cardboard gift box to carry the goodies. At the end of the sale, she was dismayed that almost everything else had been sold, except her cupcakes. Puzzled and a bit hurt, JoAnn returned home, transferred the cupcakes to a plate, and was on her way to return the cardboard lid to the shelf when she noticed neatly printed on the side of it in her own clearly legible handwriting: "Kitty's Litter Box."

—CLETE BRUMMEL

Whack! A woman hits her husband right on the head with a rolled-up magazine! "What was that for?" he shouts.

"That," she says, "was for the piece of paper I found, with the name Laurie Sue on it."

"But, dear," he says, "that was just the name of a horse I bet on when I went to the track."

"Okay," she replies. "I'll let it go, this time."

Two weeks later, *whack!*

"Now what?" he wails.

"Your horse called."

—L. ROHLENA

Item in the Cazenovia, N.Y., *Hi, Neighbor* weekly: "A resident of Fenner Street complained of a barking dog. Police investigated and found the dog to be home alone. The dog was told to keep the barking to a minimum."

—ANGELINA HARRIS

♥ ♥ ♥ ♥ ♥ ♥ ♥ ♥ ♥ ♥ ♥

The first thing I noticed about the pickup truck passing by the grocery store was the goofy-looking pooch sitting in the passenger seat wearing goggles. The second thing was the rear bumper sticker, which read:

"Dog is my copilot."

—ANNA COOPER

How many dogs does it take to change a light bulb?

- Golden retriever: "The sun is out, the day is young and you're worrying about a stupid light bulb?"
- Border collie: "Just one. And then I'll replace any wiring that's not up to code."
- Lab: "Oh, me! Me! Please let me change the bulb! Can I? Can I?"
- Rottweiler: "Make me."
- Old English sheepdog: "Light bulb? I don't see a light bulb."
- Cat: "Dogs do not change light bulbs. People change light bulbs. So the question is, how long will it be before I can expect light?"

—RICHARD WRIGHT

My local coffee shop knows how to make sure that children are well behaved. A sign advises parents: "All unattended children will be given two shots of espresso and a free puppy."

—STEPHANIE JENSEN

"Her bridge game running late again?"

❤ ❤ ❤ ❤ ❤ ❤ ❤ ❤ ❤ ❤

I once had a Saturday job in a pet shop. A young lad who'd never worked with animals before joined the staff. At closing time on his first day, I was busy tidying, so I asked him if he wouldn't mind shutting the rabbits up for me.

He emerged a while later saying he'd tried, but they weren't making that much noise anyway.

He'd been standing by the hutches saying, "Shhhhh!"

—EMMA PALMER

Traveling through New York State on a bus, I heard two men discussing their pets. One man was complaining about the powerful attraction that his female dog exercised. He claimed that on one day he counted 25 suitors in his yard. The other man remarked that they must have come from all over town.

"All over town?" exploded the dog owner, "There were two with California licenses.

—ARLENE DERETO

I am a postman. One day a colleague was delivering a package to a house, but no one was in so he pushed it through an open window. As the parcel dropped, it knocked over a goldfish bowl, which spilled onto the carpet. While wondering what to do, he saw a cat on the doorstep. He dropped the pet through the same window, hoping it would be blamed for the mess he had made.

Back at the office, my colleague found there had been a phone call to the manager. An irate neighbor wanted to know why her cat had just been pushed through her neighbor's window.

—DERRICK ROBINSON

♥ ♥ ♥ ♥ ♥ ♥ ♥ ♥ ♥ ♥ ♥

In Seattle, where a kennel license is required if you house four or more pets, a woman with two dogs and a cat called the pet-license office for information. She explained that she was considering marriage to a man with two cats and a dog.

"We both love our animals dearly and don't want to give any up," the woman said. "But if we get married, could we somehow continue to have the dogs and cats—under separate ownerships, as it were—so we wouldn't have to take out a pet-kennel license?"

The official explained that since the three dogs and three cats would be housed on the same premises, a kennel license would be required. There was a moment's silence at the other end of the line. Then, the woman said, "I think you have just stopped a wonderful marriage," and hung up abruptly.

In our neighborhood pet shop, I overheard a conversation between a mother and her young son regarding the purchase of a poodle puppy. When the mother learned that the price was $150, she gasped, grabbed her son by the hand and started out the door.

"Come on, George," she said, "you're sticking to fish."

—DELORES A. DEWHURST

One day after a nasty streak of bad weather, I asked my teenage son to take our dog out for a long walk after school. When I came home from work, I found my son stretched out on the recliner. **He had leash in hand, while the dog trotted happily away on the treadmill!**

—KAREN KELLY

♥ ♥ ♥ ♥ ♥ ♥ ♥ ♥ ♥ ♥

I was admiring a picture on my design client's wall when she came up from behind and mentioned, "That's my mother and her dog."

"She's very attractive," I said.

"She was more like a friend, really. I miss her."

"She's no longer alive?" I asked.

"No. But my mother is."

—SANDRA BOLETCHEK

An old farmer is inconsolable after his dog goes missing. His wife suggests he take out an ad in the newspaper, which he does. But two weeks later, there's still no sign of the mutt.

"What did you write in the ad?" his wife asks.

"Here, boy," he replies.

—J. LOUISE DEMCZYNA

John Bird and Bill Parrot worked in sales and marketing. One day as I was passing through their department, I heard Bill answering John's phone and wondered what the caller may have thought when he heard Bill's greeting: "Bird's line. Parrot speaking."

—ROGER D. FAY

Somewhat hard of hearing, my mother is forced to turn up the volume of her television. When I visit her, I immediately reach for the remote-control unit to turn down the racket. One day, however, our conversation was being drowned out by incessant loud singing from her pet canary, Picolo. Frustrated, mother grabbed the remote control aimed at his cage and "zapped" him.

—DENISE BROCHU

♥ ♥ ♥ ♥ ♥ ♥ ♥ ♥ ♥ ♥ ♥

At a garage sale I sampled a dab of perfume on my wrist. I loved the scent and took two bottles, but was slightly insulted by the label, which read "Dignity Dog." I brought my items to the fellow in charge, who asked me what kind of dog I had.

"I don't have a dog. Why do you ask?" I replied.

"Then why are you buying this dog-grooming formula?"

Through my embarrassment, I confessed I thought it was women's perfume, and the sale went to the dogs.

—DONNA THOMPSON

As coordinators of a school for working youths and adults in our city, we sometimes get notes from our students with excuses for their absence. One night, we were sitting in our office when one of our middle-school students asked if he could come in to explain why he'd been absent for the previous days.

"I'm getting a medical statement that justifies my absence," he began, "The reason I didn't bring it right away is because the vet didn't show up to work."

—RITA DE CÁSSIA LOPES SOARES

My wife and I were quarrelling because she thought I watched too many horror films. "Think of the effect it could be having on your mind," she complained.

"Don't be ridiculous," I scoffed and she stormed out.

She hadn't returned after several hours and, as we had guests that night, I started preparing the meal. Unfortunately, as I was chopping vegetables, the cat knocked over the pan containing my tomato sauce. I picked up the poor red-stained moggie with one hand, while holding my knife in the other. At that moment my wife walked in.

—VINCENT IWUOHA

♥ ♥ ♥ ♥ ♥ ♥ ♥ ♥ ♥ ♥ ♥

For my stepdaughter's 14th birthday, I had picked up a birthday card to be from the dog, in which I wrote numerous woofs and enclosed $50. I placed it by the front door knowing Jessica would see it before leaving for school.

In the morning my fiancée, Denine, was driving Jessica and her younger sister, Olivia, to school when Jessica opened the card and read it out loud.

"Fifty dollars!" Olivia exclaimed. "I didn't think the dog even liked you that much!"

—DAREN WESTMAN

One afternoon my six-year-old daughter showed me a picture of a fat cat she had drawn. I asked her what kind it was and she told me it was a cat that was going to have kittens. See, I'll show you, she said. Carefully she outlined in pencil four very small kittens inside the cat's body. I then asked, do you know how they got there? Looking at me seriously, she said, of course I know. I drew them.

—LINDA CLARK

On our family farm in my early teens, I had a lovely pet pig called Lizzie. Every morning Lizzie would follow me down to the paddock where I would turn on the tap. As the running water was forming a nice puddle, Lizzie would hop in and wallow and splash to her heart's content. One day I was late going to the pigpen. When I got there, Lizzie was nowhere to be found but the gate to the pen was in a mess. Lizzie had put her nose under the door, pushed it up and escaped. She was already down in the paddock. She had managed to rub against the tap, which was still running, and was busy enjoying her daily wallow in the mud and water.

—JENNY DAVIES

♥ ♥ ♥ ♥ ♥ ♥ ♥ ♥ ♥ ♥

My neighbor's dog could hardly hear, so she took him to the vet. The problem was hair in the dog's ears; once the vet removed it, the dog could hear fine. The vet then told the lady that if she wanted to keep this from reoccurring, she should buy some hair-remover lotion and rub it in her dog's ears once a month.

At the store, the druggist offered this advice: "If you're going to use the lotion under your arms, don't use deodorant for a few days."

"I'm not using it under my arms," my neighbor replied.

"Okay," the druggist said, "if you're using it on your legs, don't shave for a couple of days."

"I'm not using it on my legs, either," the lady said. "If you must know, I'm using it on my schnauzer."

"Stay off your bicycle for a week," the druggist replied.

—DARRYL MACDONALD

"I feel like a dog, Doc."
"How long has this been going on?"
"Since I was a puppy."

Our four-year-old son came home one day with a sudden interest in goldfish. After the usual lecture on caring for them, I gave in. The next time we were in the city, I took him to a pet store, and he picked out three fish. While paying for the fish, a bowl and some other necessities, I asked the salesman how long a small can of fish food would last. He looked past me at my son, who was happily shaking the fish in a plastic bag. "Probably longer than the fish," he replied.

—CLIFF WARREN

❤ ❤ ❤ ❤ ❤ ❤ ❤ ❤ ❤ ❤

After stopping at the pet store to pick up supplies for Whiskey, their dog, my sister-in-law, Kay, and her young daughter, Sheila, went to the supermarket. At the checkout, Kay couldn't figure out why she didn't have enough money to pay for the groceries. "Don't you remember, Mom?" Sheila reminded her in a loud voice. **"You spent all your money on Whiskey."**

—GERRY MCCALLUM

On Halloween, I opened the door to a child no more than four years old. As I held out the candy dish, our dog Samy came up to her, barking joyously.

"You have a dog?" said the little girl, surprised.

I told her that Samy likes children and would not hurt her. Still, she stepped back.

"Yes," she said, not reassured, "but I'm dressed as a cat!"

—MARTINE L. GONTHIER

Obviously distressed, a woman rushed up to a fellow volunteer coast guard on our local beach.

"There's a dead dog over there with its legs cut off," she said.

My colleague strode toward the spot where the body was located. He stopped short, unable to believe what he saw.

Returning to the woman, he told her, "Madam, we really do appreciate your report of the dead dog with no legs. But around here we call them seals. The little chap has just woken up and gone back into the sea."

—MIKE NEWBOLD

Also Available from Reader's Digest

Laughter, the Best Medicine

More than 600 jokes, gags, and laugh lines. Drawn from one of the most popular features of *Reader's Digest* magazine, this lighthearted collection of jokes, one-liners, and other glimpses of life is just what the doctor ordered.

ISBN 978-0-89577-977-9 • $9.95 paperback

Laughter Really Is the Best Medicine

Guaranteed to put laughter in your day, this side-splitting compilation of jokes and lighthearted glimpses of life is drawn from *Reader's Digest* magazine's most popular humor column. Poking fun at the facts and foibles of daily routines, this little volume is sure to tickle your funny bone.

ISBN 978-1-60652-204-2 • $9.95 paperback

Laughter, the Best Medicine @ Work

A laugh-out-loud collection of jokes, quotes, and quips designed to poke fun at the workplace. Laugh your way through the 9-to-5 grind with this mix of hilarious wisecracks, uproarious one-liners, and outrageous résumés. No matter how bad your day, you'll find that laughter really *is* the best medicine for all your work woes.

ISBN 978-1-60652-479-4 • $9.99 paperback

For more information, visit us at RDTradePublishing.com
E-book editions are also available.

Reader's Digest books can be purchased through retail and online bookstores. In the United States books are distributed by Penguin Group (USA) Inc. For more information or to order books, call 1-800-788-6262.